Adding a Xero to Your Practice

Practical Advice for Accountants Looking to Be Successful in the Cloud

By Doug Sleeter and Bruce Phillips

Published by

The Sleeter Group

Copyright © 2014

Product Name	Adding a Xero to Your Practice: Practical Advice for Accountants Looking to Be Successful in the Cloud
	2014
	ISBN 978-1-932487-66-4
Trademarks	Xero®, Intuit®, QuickBooks™, PracticeMaster, Needles®, TSheets, SpringAhead, BigTime, Sage Timeslips, BillQuick, Tabs3, Time Matters, Billing Matters, Amicus® Attorney, Amicus® Premium Billing, Concur Expense, Expensify, Nexonia, Constant Contact®, SmartVault®, Bill & Pay, Worldox®, and NetDocuments® trademarks or service marks are the property of their respective owners and should be treated as such.

Disclaimer	This material is intended as a learning aid. Under no circumstances shall the author or publisher be liable for any damages, including any lost profits, lost data, or other indirect damages arising out of anything written in this document or expressed directly or indirectly by the author or publisher.
Written By	Doug Sleeter and Bruce Phillips
Foreword	Rod Drury

Table of Contents

Foreword v

Preface vii

What is Xero? ix

A note about the authors x

Acknowledgements x

Chapter 1   A Chance Meeting 1

Starting on the Path 1

Chapter 2   The Paradigm Shift 7

The Traditional Paradigm for Accountants 7

Why the Old Paradigm No Longer Works 8

The History of Harshman Phillips & Company - (HPC) 12

Chapter 3   Becoming the Most Trusted and Valuable Advisor 23

What SMBs Want 23

Leverage the Role of Most Trusted to Become the Most Valuable Advisor 24

New Demands on Small Businesses Today 25

HPC Experience with SMBs 26

Chapter 4   Disruptive Trends in Small Business Accounting 33

Chunkification 34

HPC's Quest for the Holy Grail 35

Zero Entry 37

Collaborative Accounting Services............................37

Mobile 38

HPC's and Our Clients' Experience with Mobile..............40

Chapter 5   Getting over the Fear 45

Some History..46

The Internet Is the Ultimate Mainframe 48

From "Client-Centric" to "Accountant-Centric"..............49

Learning along the Way......................................50

More Opportunities for Accountants 51

Change Leadership...51

Chapter 6   Believing the Value 55

Chapter 7   Specialize for Success............................61

Should Accountants Specialize? 61

Specialization at HPC 62

Chapter 8   Agility Trumps Ability 67

Choose Agility...68

Chapter 9   There's an App for that, too: Xero's
Developer Ecosystem 73

Ecosystems Beget Product Success..........................73

What Ecosystems Must Have................................74

Bruce's Thoughts on Xero's Developer Ecosystem..............75

Chapter 10   A Few Bumps along the Road to
Success 81

Experience with Tools (Product) 81

Ease of Access...82

Security 82

Cost 83

Real-time Financial Information 83

Ability to Work from Anywhere 84

Flexibility and Scalability 84

Collaboration among Staff 84

Collaborative Consulting with Clients 85

Experience with Staff (People) 86

Experience with Workflow (Process) 89

People, Processes, and Products at HPC 92

Chapter 11   Making It Happen In Your Practice 97

1: Go Paperless 97

2. Get Rid of Your Internal Servers 98

3. Get Started with Xero 99

4. Evaluate and Educate Your Staff 100

5. Select Your Service Offerings and Target Industries 101

6. Standardize Project Management 102

7. Adopt Transparency 103

8. Go to Fixed or Value Billing 104

9. Convert Selected Clients to Xero 104

10. Work Your Niche (don't just scratch it) 105

Final thoughts 106

Appendix: Rod Drury's Webio 109

Index   111

Foreword

In all economies, small businesses are the largest contributor to growth and jobs. When we started Xero, we thought about how we can best move the needle. If we could make millions of small business owners more productive to grow opportunities for people, and make business more fun – that would be a purposeful thing to do.

Business is fun, but business owners dread doing the books. Our design-led approach allowed us to dramatically improve accounting processes. We also were excited to see the innovations arriving from all vendors and the cloud, unlocking investment into small business software.

We quickly realized that well-designed accounting software quickly evolves into a communications tool that enables accountants and bookkeepers to interact with the same accounting information at the same time, all in sync. Compliance activities start to fade away as accountants are no longer working just to get the numbers right, but become able to think about what the numbers mean.

When we met Doug and Bruce several years ago, it was a meeting of the minds. Like us, they had imagined a new way of accounting with zero data entry, and the role of the accountant changing from focusing on compliance to being a true advisor. We were excited to find industry experts who got it, and have enjoyed working with their teams in beginning to transform the industry.

We are still in the early days of the cloud software industry, and for the first time we are seeing massive investment in this space, with integrated, multivendor solutions that work seamlessly being the norm—"chunkification," as Doug would say.

These are exciting times to be the small business sector, and we are going to see more change in the next five years than we had in the past twenty-five. The cloud is operating in dog years compared to the golden age of the desktop in the nineties.

In these times of change, having navigators like Doug and Bruce guiding you through this exciting journey is vital, and this book is your best resource to get started.

We look forward to working with you for many years to come as we reimagine what is possible for small business owners around the world.

Rod Drury

CEO, Xero
@roddrury

Preface

The two of us have spent the past twenty years on the bleeding edge of change in the accounting profession. As one of the nation's premier accounting technology experts (Doug), and as one of the most successful Xero accountants in the U.S. (Bruce), we want to share with you not only what we know about the changes that are sweeping the profession, but also how to take advantage of the opportunities they represent.

Throughout this book, Doug will share insights into how to be successful in this changing environment, and Bruce will share how his practice, Harshman Phillips & Company (HPC), has already walked the path and learned many lessons along the way.

If you are like many accountants, you have started to feel it. The tremors that let you know something big is coming. A seismic shift in the accounting profession is under way, and as the ground begins to shake, keeping your footing could become difficult. Just like an earthquake destroys virtually everything in a town, these fundamental shifts could be devastating to many traditional accounting practices if the firm owners fail to act.

In this book, we provide insights about how to avoid becoming a casualty, but more importantly, we'll do our best to show you how to create a firm that thrives in the new world. We will talk not just about adding Xero technology to your practice, but also about adding a zero to your profitability.

The book is divided into the following chapters.

Chapter One, A Chance Meeting, is Bruce's story about his "aha" moment in 2011, and how that put him on the path to building a 21st century accounting firm based on Xero technology.

Chapter Two, The Paradigm Shift, is Doug's description of how virtually everything in small business technology and the practice of accounting is changing, and how traditional models for accounting services are now virtually obsolete. Bruce shares the history of his firm's experience practicing in the old paradigm, and how it prepared him for the new.

Chapter Three, Becoming the Most Trusted and Most Valuable Advisor, reveals some key research done by The Sleeter Group about what owners of small and medium sized business (SMBs) want from their accountant, and how new cloud-based solutions open the door for you to do more for your clients. Bruce shares how his practice has taken on this role with its clients.

Chapter Four, Disruptive Trends in Small Business Accounting, includes Doug's views on the impact of four game changing trends in small business accounting: chunkification, zero entry, collaborative accounting services, and mobile technology. Bruce discusses how his firm has incorporated these ideas into its practice.

Chapter Five, Getting over the Fear, puts the current period of disruption into historical context and discusses how the shifts present opportunities not seen in decades for accountants.

Chapter Six, Believing the Value, offers thoughts and advice about believing in yourself and the value you create.

Chapter Seven, Specialize for Success, focuses on how specialization in specific business types allows your firm to deepen your relationships with clients and provide a broader range of services. Bruce shares how specialization benefitted his firm and its clients.

Chapter Eight, Agility Trumps Ability, is Doug's challenge to you to think differently about your processes and the tools you use to serve clients. Bruce shares the decisions his company made that prioritized agility, and how that helped them embrace the future.

Chapter Nine, There's an App for that: Xero's Developer Ecosystem, discusses Doug's views of the importance of add-ons for designing a complete small business accounting system. Bruce discusses how he integrated several add-ons into his practice.

Chapter Ten, A Few Bumps along the Road to Success, covers all of the lessons Bruce learned throughout this process.

And finally, **Chapter Eleven**, Making it Happen in Your Practice, covers the steps involved with creating a truly innovative, 21st century accounting firm using Xero and the Xero ecosystem of add-on software.

What is Xero?

Xero (www.xero.com) is online accounting software for small businesses. Built from the start for the cloud, you can log in anywhere, anytime from any device. It offers 24-7 real-time cash flow information and up-to-the-minute financials. It connects directly with your data sources, such as your banks, customers, and other small business applications.

Features include:

- General Ledger, AR, AP, payroll, and reporting
- Easy bank reconciliation
- Fully native mobile app with full functionality
- An ecosystem of over 350 third-party add-on apps
- Unlimited users

Xero is a global company with over 371,000 paying customers in over 100 countries.

A note about the authors

Throughout this book, you will hear from both Doug and Bruce individually and from the two of us together. When we refer to "we" we are referring to the both of us. You will also hear from Bruce directly in the stories he shares from his practice. We identify these stories in the heading of the section. There will also be times when either of us shares something individually in first person. In these cases, we identify whose words you are reading.

Acknowledgements

Doug Sleeter

It takes a team of people to make a book come to life, and I want to thank the whole team for helping us push this book out in near-record time. Of course, the biggest thanks goes to my co-author Bruce Phillips. He's a true friend, and his enthusiasm for everything he does is contagious to all who come to know him. He's successful on purpose, and I've learned a lot from him through our working together. As you read this book, you'll learn a lot about success from him too.

Rod Drury, CEO and Founder of Xero, deserves so much thanks, not only for creating such a great company and product (even though he says the name has nothing to do with the zero-entry trend I talk about in chapter four), but also because he helped both Bruce and I immensely along the way. Rod, your support means everything, so as you say, thanks for that.

I also want to thank the whole team at the Xero US headquarters. We received incredible support throughout the project from Ian Vacin, Vice President of Product Strategy and Marketing. He not only helped us with early concepts, but helped us immensely during the development process. Also, Jamie Sutherland, President of Xero US has been a true friend of The Sleeter Group throughout, and I thank him for everything he's done for us.

I can't leave out a thank you to all the great staff at The Sleeter Group (sleeter.com), including the contractors who have helped us get this project done. Deborah Pembrook spearheaded the project, and provided both Bruce and me with great feedback, suggestions, and overall encouragement to make this a book that really delivers value to our readers. Thanks Deborah! Others who provided exactly the right help at the right time are Jeannie Ruesch, Charlie Russell, Greg Lam, Misty Megia, and T.M. Hawley who was the copy editor of the book. You guys rock!

Last, but maybe most importantly, I thank my wife and business partner Sherrill and my son Tom for reading every word and telling me what they think without sugar coating. I really thrive on that, and I thank them dearly for just telling me like it is.

Bruce Phillips

It would not have been possible to write this book without the help and support of many of the people around me and in my world, only some of whom is it possible to mention here.

First and foremost, I would like to express my deepest gratitude to Doug Sleeter, for his patient guidance, enthusiastic encouragement, excellent ideas, and useful critiques of this book. His willingness to give his time so generously is very much appreciated. I also thank my main contact at the Sleeter Group on the project, Deborah Pembrook, for her valuable guidance and advice. She inspired me greatly to work on this book, and was instrumental in bringing the whole story together. I also appreciate the assistance and patience provided by the rest of the staff at The Sleeter Group. They were awesome to work with.

My completion of this project and having the successes and stories to tell could not have been accomplished without many other important people. The advice and counsel, generous support, and friendship of almost my entire career, many thanks go out to my former partner, Bill Harshman, the co-founder of Harshman Phillips & Company (hpccpa.com). Others, such as Brett Baker and Roger Landry, taught me a lot about having partners who could be truly trusted such as you are. And Tony Halligan, for believing in me in the early days.

I cannot express enough thanks to Rod Drury, CEO of Xero, and to the entire Xero team all over the United States. Their continuous support was instrumental in helping with the success that led to the opportunity to even write this book. I value some of the deepest and long-lasting friendships that came out of our relationships.

My special thanks are extended to the staff and team of HPC including Jen Huang, Ann Dykes, Sharon Garrett, Sam Thomas, Mike Vanecek, Dianne McLeod, and Stephanie Boyd for allowing me time away from you to research and write. YOU are the reason HPC has had the success that it has.

A very special thank you to my wife, Maggie, without whom none of this would have been possible. Her taking care of virtually everything, including the HPC team, and me, while I wrote, traveled, and built the practice and took care of business, will always mean the world to me. Words cannot express how truly grateful and lucky I have been.

Finally, I also would like to thank the others who helped inspire me when the writing became difficult. You know who you are. Without your help, the story may never have been told.

Chapter 1
A Chance
Meeting

Starting on the Path
Bruce's Story

It all started with a chance meeting.

A few years ago, I left my traditional accounting practice in Atlanta and risked everything on a tech start-up in LA. At first it was like a dream. I was working for a company and product I truly believed in. We had top clients, such as Walt Disney and Freemantle Media. And I was living right off the beach in Playa del Rey. I not only worked long hours but also invested heavily. I thought we were on our way to building something fantastic.

But in 2008, the venture capital didn't come through and the economy took that turn. The company continued to make a go of it, but I couldn't see a way to make it thrive. Finally, my wife told me she was going back to Atlanta—and that it was up to me if I were to go with her.

I returned to my accounting firm in Atlanta, determined to change how we did things. I had seen how technology was changing the world, and I wanted to be a part of it. Wasn't there a way to bring fresh ideas and new ways of doing things into the accounting field? Perhaps I could help expand our accounting services in ways that would allow us to better serve our clients and increase our revenue.

I knew I needed to talk to the most innovative thinkers in the profession. Throwing caution to the wind, I declared myself a "sponge" and spent a year travelling the country talking with thought leaders in our industry, and exploring everything from QuickBooks to Intacct. I learned about hosting and software as a service (SaaS). I talked with all kinds of vendors who supported accounting, and to other firms moving to the cloud. Then, I picked what I considered to be the best of breed in every category. But no matter how I tried, everything was clunky and slow (not to mention expensive). I wanted to fall in love, but everything I tried just felt like settling.

But then I had that chance meeting I mentioned above. It changed everything for me and my practice.

I met Rod Drury, the founder of Xero, at The Sleeter Group's 2011 Accounting Solutions Conference in Las Vegas. He spoke, I listened, and I realized that some technology like Xero was going to dramatically change the way accountants interact with their clients.

I saw that Xero was elegant. It was built solely for the cloud, has direct connections to banks, and has the capability of using real-time data. As I looked deeper into Xero, there was just one thought going through my mind.

"I think this is the solution I've been looking for."

It was then that I decided that my practice would change the way we did everything. I flew back to Atlanta as if on a mission, and immediately set up Harshman Phillips & Company (HPC) on Xero. Within six months, we were Xero's number-one partner in the United States.

Throughout this book, I'll share with you how I took my practice from the old paradigm to the new, and how those changes made my practice more successful and profitable.

None of this would have been possible if I hadn't flown from Atlanta to Las Vegas, and Rod hadn't flown from New Zealand to the United States. Sometimes a chance meeting is all it takes to send you out on your true path.

The best way to predict the future is to create it.

Peter Drucker

Chapter 2
The Paradigm
Shift

The Traditional Paradigm for Accountants

As we write this book in mid-2014, we are continuing to see a complete paradigm shift in accounting technology and the relationships between accountants and their clients.

Over the past few years, we've seen several emerging trends that are at the core of the paradigm shift. These trends are what I, Doug, refer to as "chunkification" of the business process, zero data entry, collaborative accounting services, and the explosion of mobile devices and mobile access to data.

We will talk about those trends in detail later on. But before we do, let's dissect the "old world" we've been living in for the past thirty years or so. That was how accountants worked with clients, and the business model (or paradigm) that developed around that old way of doing things.

The old world was characterized by accountants and clients working separately in their own offices, and using different software and data. Their communication took all sorts of forms—sometimes telephone, sometimes in-person meetings, and recently sometimes as email and text messages.

In that world, we all built out our offices with desktops, LANs, and servers. Accountants and clients alike had pretty much the same hardware and software infrastructure, and of course they all incurred the costs associated with that infrastructure. Even today, most businesses have Windows servers in the back room that are connected to desktops via LANs. When a firm used remote workers, they had to install additional infrastructure to support those activities. And then there were the costs to maintain those systems. That included IT staffing, software updates, monitoring security issues such as antivirus and firewalls, and troubleshooting networking issues, software incompatibilities, driver updates, and all those pesky details that needed attention to keep the offices running smoothly.

Why the Old Paradigm No Longer Works

Accountants are isolated from client data.

Data is locked up at clients' offices where clients enter it on their own and later bring the resulting mess to the accountant for financial statement prep and tax returns. This is inefficient at best, and completely unsustainable in the new world, where people demand instant access to information.

While many of the technologies we've been using for the past thirty years have served us quite well, the velocity of change in the business world has increased pressure on small businesses to keep up with customer demands. Your clients' customers now assume they can work with every business via the Internet. Similarly, clients assume they can work with their accounting firm via the Internet.

In addition to working with clients via the Internet, new business models for accountants must align with what clients *really* want from us, and that goes far beyond the compliance services of tax and accounting. In short, we need to become what we've always said we were—the most trusted advisor.

Think about the clients' data. In most cases, small-business clients store their live data—the accounting software master data file, such as the QuickBooks QBW file or the Customer Relationship Management (CRM) database—at their offices in desktops or servers. Of course, the accountant sometimes needs to work on that data. Essentially, the accountant's work product of data analysis, presentation of financial statements, tax returns, and so forth is all about the clients' data. But when the live data is sitting on the servers in the clients' offices, we have a choice. Accountants can travel to the clients' offices and do the work there, or maybe remotely log into the client's servers and work on it. Of course, this is not very convenient, and there are significant complexities with getting this to work reliably. Nevertheless, there are ways to make this work using products like GoToMyPC, LogMeIn, and Windows Remote Desktop.

But since most accountants prefer to work in their own offices, the old world way of working with clients' data was to take copies of it and work on the copies at the accounting office.

This whole paradigm is a problem. Think about the cost, complexity, inconvenience, risk of data loss, security risk, and overall inefficiency of working this way.

Cost: Both client and accountant must invest in the same hardware and software, so it's expensive. If we were to have only one investment in hardware and software, wouldn't that be less costly overall?

Complexity: The paradigm is complex because the software, firewalls, and security settings to remotely access client servers often require an IT support person to set up and manage.

Inconvenience: It is extremely inconvenient for accountants and clients because accountants must coordinate with clients about when to work remotely or when they'll come and take copies of the data.

Risk of data loss: If accountants take copies of client data, there is a pretty significant risk of data loss. Data could get out of sync when the accountant takes copies of the data and starts working on it, while clients are continuing to enter transactions into their copy of the data. Of course there are best practices to avoid this situation, but even with all the tricks, the complexities get in the way and often there is some mix-up that causes data loss because the copies of the data get out of sync.

Security risk: If accountants have copies of client data files on their servers, there is a significant security issue. Pause a minute and think about what's in that data file. It's not just a couple of debits and credits in the general ledger. The client's accounting data file has all the employee addresses, phone numbers, social security numbers, and maybe the customer list has each customer's credit card number. Every business is required to keep this information strictly confidential, and protect it from data breaches. If you're an accountant, we doubt you would ever want to assume the risk of a security breach of client data. Maybe a burglar gets in and steals all the hard drives, or a hacker penetrates the accounting office network. If there is a breach, you have actually caused your clients to fail in their responsibilities to their customers and employees.

Inefficiency: Finally, the overall inefficiency of working this way just doesn't make sense, given that there are compelling alternatives. In the old world, we didn't have good options like we now have with cloud-based servers. We simply had to make our whole business model work given the paradigm of client-centric accounting software, located on client servers, and not easily accessible by the accountant.

Ever since the PC revolution, the accounting profession has moved *further away* from being a partner in the business to being more of a servant who provides commoditized services.

It's clear to me that the paradigm shift is changing virtually everything about how people work and communicate. How will you incorporate this shift into your business? If you're not yet feeling the pain of how the old world is holding you back, I predict you will soon.

Not to scare you, but in many ways, this paradigm shift is like a freight train. It might feel like it's far away and it's hard to really tell how fast it's going, but it's clear to me that no accounting professional can afford to wait and see how things work out. You must embrace these changes and incorporate them into your practice or risk a decline in your client base that will surely accelerate the longer you delay. In a sense, if you don't transform your practice into a 21st century practice, your competitors will, and your clients will notice. Which side of the curve do you want to be on? Do you want to add a zero, or risk subtracting one?

The History of Harshman Phillips & Company - (HPC)
Bruce's Story

Here is the story of how I and my company came to embrace the paradigm shift and build a successful 21st century practice, centered on Xero.

Bill Harshman and I have been through quite a bit together and although there have been lots of distractions (mostly on my end), we've stuck together and made things work very well for over two decades. I owe him a lot for always being there through thick and thin. Our practice started out in 1992 with three partners working around a conference table and we grew to twenty-two people by the late nineties.

Here is the story of how we got together and how that developed into such a successful partnership.

After growing up in Rhode Island in the 1970s and attending the College of William & Mary from 1980 to 1984, I decided to go south to Atlanta. It was an up and coming city, and I saw potential for career growth as well as nice weather.

I started my career with Arthur Young in Atlanta in 1983 and later became an audit manager for Ernst & Young in the late 1980s.

One of the largest clients of Arthur Young's Atlanta office was Lockheed, the manufacturer of large aircraft such as the C-5 Galaxy and C-130 transport planes. Since I've loved airplanes my whole life I asked to be assigned to the Lockheed account. I started out doing grunt work in late 1983 and early 1984, but after a few years I was running the whole job and loving it. I learned everything there was to know about costing large manufacturing projects, in this case airplanes. We used lots and the most complicated overhead allocations I have ever seen. I also learned how to do revenue recognition when you had no idea how much revenue you were eventually going to receive. Not to mention the possibility that the government may change or cancel their order whenever the winds blew the wrong way.

In addition to spending about four months each year on the Lockheed account, I spent about five months each year working on the Arrow Shirt Company account. It was a very popular brand but a great brand doesn't mean you will have automatic success. Arrow struggled and was eventually purchased by West Point-Pepperell, another Arthur Young Atlanta office client.

For the next several years, I stayed deeply involved with Arrow Shirt Company (involved in mergers and acquisitions), as companies and divisions were bought and sold.

I finally left Ernst & Young for two reasons. One was that the firm pre-merger (Arthur Young) was very different from the firm after the merger (Ernst & Young). In Atlanta, Ernst & Whinney was much larger than Arthur Young, which was the smallest of the big eight. Arthur Young felt like a small company (at least in Atlanta) where everyone in the office knew each other. My department, auditing, had about fifty employees.

The second reason I left was that I loved my job. I had two large clients at the firm, but that limited my exposure to the partners and other institutional knowledge. I knew that if I was to ever grow in my career, I needed to have a wider perspective. Since I couldn't give up those two clients, I decided it was time to look elsewhere.

About that time, for some strange reason, I decided to learn the tax code. I believed that the only way to ever be self-sufficient was to be able to advise on taxes. Even now as we provide client accounting services, many of the inquiries and prospects ask tax-related questions. Being able to answer those questions confidently and on the spot makes a huge difference.

Continuing my search for the next opportunity, I answered an ad from a boutique CPA firm in Atlanta, Halligan & Associates. During the interview with Tony Halligan, I learned that he was looking for two people: one to help run and take care of his audit department, and one to help with business development. I also got the impression that he was starting to look at a succession plan, as there had been some turmoil at his firm over the past few years, including the departure of a couple of partners. Although I can't imagine why I had the confidence to say so, I told Tony that I could do it all. I had never sold anything, I didn't have any clients of my own, and I had never brought any new clients to Arthur Young or Ernst & Young.

Of course, bringing in new clients was obviously more difficult at a large firm that commanded big fees and had large overhead costs, but I thought I would be a good salesman, and I never had any doubt that I could improve the audit department and allow Tony to focus on other things. Eventually he offered me the job at $60,000 year (a lot for a manager in the early nineties) and the promise of a ten-percent partnership on my one-year anniversary.

I will never forget going to the head of the audit department at Ernst & Young to announce I was leaving. It was really hard because I loved it there (before the merger), and I loved working with all those good people. Also, I learned a ton and I built several long-lasting friendships.

As a boutique firm, Halligan had a few marquee clients. I was fortunate enough to be able work on and manage them, since they all happened to be audit clients. I was watching and learning everything I could about how to build and maintain client relationships. Little did I realize then how important that would become a year later.

On March 17, 1992, about a year and a half after I started with Tony, he had a heart attack and unfortunately passed the same day. He was driving back from his annual St. Patrick's Day ritual in Savannah. At the time, the firm had two minority partners who each held a ten-percent interest. Losing the founder and face of the firm on March 17, in the middle of tax season, was devastating for everyone associated with the firm, not only from a business perspective, but also personally. I was thirty years old, and had found a mentor and a path for the rest of my career. He was a great tax guy, could manage the audits, and all of his partners, clients, and employees loved him.

Not sure what to do, and wanting to prevent a mass exodus of the marquee clients (and the rest of the clients, for that matter), I called Bill Harshman. He had left Ernst & Young I believe in early 1991 and was practicing on his own. I didn't know Bill all that well, other than seeing him in the office on weekends with his then very young kids who liked to play under his desk. We had worked together on a few clients, and I knew he was a tremendous tax practitioner. He could quote tax code sections verbatim, and he had everybody's respect.

But none of that had anything to do with why I called him. The reason I called was because I had felt a connection with

him a couple of years before when I was just leaving Ernst &
Young. When heard I was leaving, he asked me to lunch and
we got to know each other and felt a synergy that I wanted to
recapture. That was the start of a twenty-two-year
partnership.

I asked Bill to come in that third week of March and help
with some of the bigger tax clients. He agreed to join and it
turned out well for both of us because these were very good
clients who needed his expertise and could afford to pay our
fees. Even to this day, Bill has maintained business and
personal relationships with some of these clients.

Bill and I worked together for several months until things
calmed down. Fortunately, we lost only one large client
during the aftermath of Tony's death. I was determined to
keep *all* the clients, but even after a long lunch with the
CEO/Founder in which I gave it my best shot, I realized that
there was nothing I (a mere thirty year old) could do. I clearly
wasn't Tony Halligan. But I did learn a very valuable lesson.
Relationships matter!

After about three months of working together, Bill and I
decided that we could give it a go for the long haul. It was a
good pairing because he had deep tax experience and I had
extensive audit experience. His "gray hair," as we called it at
the time, combined with my youth and personality also made
for a great team. We tried to buy Halligan & Associates from
Tony Halligan's estate, but we couldn't make that work. In
fact, just a few months after our attempt to purchase, one of
the attorneys involved came into my office and told me to
clean out my desk, and then he escorted me off the premises.
As it turned out, though, I had the last laugh. Three of the

firm's top four clients said they would follow me whatever I choose to do. *Relationships matter!*

How much do relationships matter? I am still doing business with two of those clients today. Over the years, one of them expanded internationally, so I had the opportunity to travel and learn about doing business overseas. I owe that client a lot. Our relationship is so special that I spent the last two Christmases with his family at their lodge.

Since we couldn't buy Tony's practice, Bill and I decided to just put our clients together and start our own. We shared space with another former partner at Arthur Young, and we started off working out of a small conference room. I remember putting together the initial budget in which we decided to take monthly draws of a thousand dollars. We promised ourselves we would increase it as soon as we could. The good news was that it didn't take long for us to start earning ten thousand a month, all the while building our staff, getting our own space, and starting to create what eventually became HPC.

The firm operated as a traditional CPA firm doing audit, tax, and advisory services. We had a few new partners come and go along the way. Having a deep-rooted entrepreneurial spirit, I occasionally lost focus but always came back to my core each time.

One of my "lost focus" events was when a friend approached me with an idea of starting a construction company. He already had a couple of large contracts to build multifamily apartments, but he needed some capital and a partner. He asked me to help him find a partner and funding. I decided I would be that funding and partner. Roger, a good ol' Louisiana boy from Lake Charles, and I put together a deal structure to borrow money from some of my clients. I put my own money in with that and raised $500,000 of working capital for Roger to use for our new construction company, GWL Construction.

Each of the loans was secured by the membership interests in GWL Construction, and personally guaranteed by me. I figured there was no way I would ever let any of my clients lose money, so I might as well guarantee it. Each investor received fifteen percent annual interest, paid monthly. Again, I figured if I gave them a check each month for their interest, that would be a good thing. So, Roger paid distributions each month to me, and I turned around and paid the interest. At the end of day, everybody made fifteen percent on their money, plus a couple of extension fees. More importantly, everyone received every dollar they invested back. The construction company had revenues of about $80,000,000 over a three-year period. Everyone was very happy and we all made lots of money. This lesson was, don't be afraid to be creative and try new things. I had never done anything like that before. But I worked with people who trusted each other. Note the word "trust." Like relationships, trust is another thing that matters.

The construction business was so lucrative at the time, we decided to branch out. Roger and I figured that if we did this, we could do the associated real estate development. So we started a real estate development company. We even leveraged our expertise about the tax credit opportunities associated with the properties. We figured they had to be sold, so why not buy them ourselves, and sell them at a profit? So we put together an entity to buy and sell the tax credits from the property we had developed and built.

The last piece was the real estate management. No reason to miss that one. So Roger started a management company to manage the properties that we developed, built, and financed. You are probably seeing a pattern here. We kept learning and were willing to try new things. We built a pretty successful enterprise.

During this time, I learned about vertical and horizontal integration. The concept was to never leave anything on the table. That lesson weaves through our current business today, as you will see later in the chapter about building out your service offerings and bundling them together.

After my education in construction, real estate, fundraising, and tax credits, I switched my focus to finding ways to leverage technology to improve efficiencies across all businesses. That was when the light bulb came on and gave me the courage to make dramatic changes at HPC.

One of my physician clients had invested in a tech start-up, and asked me what I thought. When I started to check into it, little did I suspect that it would lead to a career change and be the catalyst for so many other developments. Since the start-up was in the digital media space, the first thing I did was to call on a digital media expert and long-time friend to evaluate the company with me. He and I were so impressed that we both became investors and he became the COO. But first I had to get the capital and legal structure cleaned up, so I went to work on that. After understanding the business model, believing in it, and trusting the founder, I invested more of my own money. I was going all in.

Eventually, we moved the company to Los Angeles because that was where our customers were. We were doing business with Walt Disney, Endemol, and FreemantleMedia. Endemol was the producer of *Deal or No Deal,* and Freemantle produced *American Idol.* These customers were the real deal, and being in Los Angeles was fun. Traveling back and forth for six months and living in an extended-stay hotel, not so much. So I rented a condo, shipped my convertible out, and convinced my wife to join me. All was good.

The only issue was that we were always trying to raise venture capital. We must have met with fifty firms. Unfortunately, our CEO, who was rather wealthy, was funding the company himself. And because of that, we never were able to raise outside capital. This is what I call "funding to fail." Always covering payroll, but never providing enough to truly succeed.

Working with the digital media company taught me not to be afraid of technology. I had always thought I was pretty tech savvy, but in hindsight, I now see that I wasn't, really.

Building out websites and back-end systems, learning the basics of coding, datacenters, operating and testing environments, and of course comprehending the infrastructure behind it all, including servers, firewalls, switches, and security (both physical and access) was an eye opener to say the least.

That hard-won expertise in technology was the catalyst that allowed me to pay attention to Rod Drury when I met him in late 2011. All of my professional experience to that point had given me the courage to shake things up and take some chances.

In a time of drastic change, it is learners who inherit the future.

Eric Hoffer

Chapter 3 Becoming the Most Trusted and Valuable Advisor

What SMBs Want

In January 2014, The Sleeter Group conducted a survey to find out what small and medium-sized businesses (SMBs) wanted from their CPAs. The survey revealed significant gaps between what SMBs wanted and what they have been receiving from their accountants. It also uncovered some surprising ways that SMBs rank the criteria they use for selecting a CPA.

What I, Doug, found most surprising is that "proactive strategic advice" was the third-highest-rated factor, with an average score of 8.7 out of 10, coming in ahead of "reputation" and "low fees" (Figure 1). The fact that proactive strategic advice rated so high shows SMBs want a CPA who is a partner in their success, one who thinks often and strategically about their business. Proactive strategic advice can be what is most obvious, business and/or tax planning, but it can also take the form of technology planning to improve the efficiency of a business's operations. Simple recommendations, such as a solution for online document sharing or associating electronic documents with accounting transactions, can go a long way toward solidifying the perception of the CPA as a proactive strategic partner.

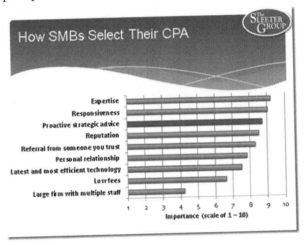

Figure 1: Criteria SMBs use to choose a CPA

Leverage the Role of Most Trusted to Become the Most Valuable Advisor

In the new paradigm, public practitioners must build business models that are dramatically broader in scope (more services) and deeper in focus (more client- and process-oriented).

The successful accountant significantly broadens and deepens his or her relationship with each client to help those clients achieve *what they want,* not just what they need.

In the new world, the meaning of "most trusted advisor" is changing. Now that we can collaborate with clients and access their data in real time, we have amazing opportunities that allow us to:

- Move from being isolated to being present with each client.

- Take a leadership role with our clients, in which we help them find tailored solutions that fit their needs.
- Turn our relationship from serving to *partnering* for success.
- Leverage the reputation of being the most trusted advisor to become the most *valuable* advisor.

New Demands on Small Businesses Today

For those accountants and SMBs who rely on desktop accounting software such QuickBooks, Sage 50, MYOB, or any of the dozens of Windows-based systems, there is a whole new wave of solutions coming to market and disrupting the small-business accounting software industry.

These innovations are attracting venture capital and beginning to deliver productivity improvements for those SMBs who have been increasingly frustrated by the limitations of desktop software from the old paradigm. As you'll see from the examples below, the web and mobile world addresses SMB customer demand in ways that outstrip the functionality of yesterday's desktop software.

Examples:

- Customers demand the opportunity to do business online, including shopping, ordering, documentation, and support.
- Businesses with multiple locations need instant access to sales activity, inventory levels, and support activity.
- Businesses that sell products face increasingly complex tax environments for calculating, remitting, and reporting sales taxes. Without web-based solutions, compliance costs are too high for most SMBs.

- Employees want direct deposit for paychecks, and online access to paystubs and W-2s.

- Customers, vendors, employees, and management all want access to mission-critical data from mobile devices.

HPC Experience with SMBs
Bruce's Story

Over the more than two years since July, 2012, when HPC put its first paying client on Xero, I have personally spoken with more than 600 SMBs, addressing their inquiries about HPC cloud-based Xero services. Having listened to each of them tell me his or her story, several things became clear.

First, they all wanted a cloud-based accounting product with services wrapped around it, a solution that leveraged the power of real-time data. In many cases, however, I think they really didn't understand what that power would mean for them. For example, some didn't realize that an accountant and a client, in separate locations, could look at the same data at the same time. And what's more, this would allow us to not only answer specific questions, but also correct or modify a client's books during the course of a telephone conversation or video conference.

Second, many of them had not been getting proactive advice; that was why they were reaching out to another CPA. And they wanted someone to explain Xero and how it could work in their practice, even though many had already heard or read about it. I was more than willing to comply. In my opinion, the reason they were not getting proactive advice was their old CPA was stuck in the old paradigm: after-the-fact bookkeeping (and many times, way after the fact). How can you possibly help your client make sound business decisions when they receive their financial statements too late for them to do anything about what the statements are telling them?

Another thing that I noticed since mid-2012 is a change in the types of calls and emails that we have received. In the beginning, people were asking us to explain what cloud software was all about, what Xero was about, and how it compared to other products on the market. But now, more of our calls and emails reflect an understanding of all that, and begin with an assumption that they're going to Xero. They call us to find out how we, as top advisors, can help them implement it in their situation.

What HPC did was to continually tweak our business model to deal with the top three desires of SMBs according to the Sleeter survey. (Not that we needed the survey to tell us these things. We figured them out on our own by virtue of our interest in continually improving our relationships with our clients.) Our clients want expertise, responsiveness, and proactive strategic advice. So that is what we have been focusing on, and they just happened to coincide with the top responses in the survey.

We will deal first with expertise. It began with figuring out what we were really good at. When we started out, we took any type of client, as long as they wanted a cloud solution and were a good fit for Xero. If we thought we could help them automate their processes, and there was potential for things working out well for us too, we took them on. We took many that we expected to be learning experiences. And boy, did we learn. Maybe the most important thing we learned was that specialization is the key. We just took a long way to get there, but we also learned a lot about the different types of businesses that we never would have learned otherwise. We did everything from retail to e-commerce, professional services, software developers, venture capital firms, private equity, and nonprofit. Each one had its own unique accounting and back office needs. They could be inventory, sales tax, data from shopping carts, etc. The point is, once we learned about which businesses we could really help and how we could help them, we modified our business model. In this case, we learned how to provide expertise by finding our niches.

The second-most desired characteristic was responsiveness. We had never really had an issue with that, but we also understood that clients who use the cloud and communicate in the new world typically expect responses pretty fast, virtually immediately. So the mantra of "return all phone calls (or emails) within 24 hours" wasn't going to cut it anymore. Consequently, we began to provide unlimited phone and email support to all of our Xero clients. While we don't currently include a response time as part of our engagement letter or service-level agreement, it is our policy that when a client asks for something, they get it as soon as possible, and definitely the same day.

This has gone over big. We even make sure that our entrepreneurial clients, who are difficult to communicate with because they are all very busy, hear from us every month. They know we are here, reviewing their Xero files, and available if they need us. Another thing we figured out was to communicate with each client by their preferred means. It always surprises me, but we have a few clients who really don't want to talk on the phone. Email is their preference. I am not sure if they just want the trail that email provides, or if it is more for the convenience. What I can tell you is, I hate getting tons of voicemails. I would much rather get emails.

Reason? Because I can respond when I want to. That could be midnight. Can't return a phone call then. There definitely is something to this.

The third characteristic was proactive strategic advice. On this front, we did two things. On the accounting side, we offered a controller or virtual CFO to many of our clients who were receiving support-level or bookkeeping services. By giving them access to someone who not only reconciles their bank and credit card statements, and prepares their financial statements, but also explains what those documents mean, and does many other things besides, we were in effect providing advice, and thus paving our way to becoming their most trusted advisor. All this was possible due to 1) real-time access to data, 2) collaborative tools such as Skype, GoToMeeting, and Lync, and 3) having the right people.

Luck is what happens when preparation meets opportunity.

Seneca

Chapter 4
Disruptive Trends in Small Business Accounting

Since about 2010, we've seen four trends that I, Doug, believe will fundamentally change the way small business owners, bookkeepers, accountants, and even taxing agencies will use technology in their everyday activities.

Some will conclude that these technology shifts are not altogether positive, but I believe they will prove their usefulness regardless of their effect on any specific metric, and therefore warrant our focus and understanding. In fact, the definition of "disruptive" technology implies that the new solutions will displace earlier solutions.

These four trends are:

Chunkification: Splitting up overall business management systems into discrete parts.

Zero Entry: Removing, to the extent possible, the task of entering data into a general ledger or other financial record. This takes advantage of connections between the chunks, moves us closer to a zero-entry world, and dramatically changes the role of the bookkeeper.

Collaborative Accounting Services: Providing accounting services that make the most of the electronic connections between accountants and their clients. Being able to work on the same data facilitates much tighter relationships.

Mobile: Taking the fullest possible advantage of mobile technology. Access to information from a variety of mobile devices allows us to rethink the possible, and developers are scrambling to capitalize on this new reality.

Now let's look closely at each of the trends.

Chunkification

In the past thirty years or so, the accounting software market has been dominated by large, all-in-one accounting products such as QuickBooks; Sage 50, 100, and 300; Microsoft Dynamics; and others. All of these products include the functions that SMBs need: functions such as general ledger, accounts receivable, accounts payable, payroll, inventory, and reporting. While those products were built to solve the horizontal needs of clients by providing basic features common to all businesses, most did not provide the vertical, industry-specific customizations needed by nearly every SMB.

The new crop of solutions, nearly all of which are online applications, are "chunkifying" those large systems into specific business processes to provide more specific functionality and verticalization. This is, however, a double-edged sword. On the one hand, it's great because we can now match specific business processes to specific clients, but on the other hand, we now have to worry more about how each of the chunks will fit together into a unified accounting system.

Nevertheless, chunkification of business processes is compelling. With the broad adoption of the cloud and mobile devices, developers can now focus on the deep functionality and integration that customers demand. And by focusing on smaller chunks, they can develop more profitable business models that allow them to continually improve, update, and customize their solutions to meet the evolving demands of the market. Clients gain amazing benefits from this chunkification because they can pick the best matches for the individual parts of their accounting systems, instead of having to compromise with the warts in some areas of whichever product they choose.

Some examples of chunkification are:

- Shopping carts and web stores
- Point-of-sale software that connects to back-end accounting systems
- Document management systems in a secure online vault, with links to accounting transactions, customer relationship management (CRM) records, etc.
- CRM software
- Online invoicing and bill payment solutions

HPC's Quest for the Holy Grail
Bruce's Story

When considering the disruptive trends in small-business accounting, we see that for many years people were looking for what I call the Holy Grail—a single solution that would satisfy all our needs in one software package or suite. Well, HPC's quest for this Holy Grail was not always sunshine and roses. It meant finding a monolithic system that could handle taxes, accounting, practice management, document management, portals, research, email, etc. all in a software suite that worked seamlessly.

The two big players in our industry, Thomson and CCH, were leading accountants to believe that they could provide such a Holy Grail. But back in 2008, it didn't work exactly the way they had been selling it. We tried it by using the virtual office (VO) from Thomson, and from my perspective, they sold us a bill of goods; it went very badly. We had to migrate all our email off our Microsoft Exchange Server, and everything else, onto their VO. But within 30 days, we found out that it didn't work the way we had been told it would. So then we had to move all of our email back onto an AppRiver server, which turned out to be a very good decision. Getting rid of our Microsoft Exchange Server, and whole VO experience, were very painful.

But we learned a valuable lesson. We had thought we were very smart about what we were doing, but what we didn't know was the right questions to ask.

I believe many of you are in the same boat that we were in: owning an expensive system that doesn't do what you need it to. Fortunately, with the widespread adoption of web technologies and software as a service (SaaS), it became obvious that systems needed to work together and talk with each other. So it was going to be okay to use specialized software packages that were not part of some monolithic suite. Open API infrastructure is largely responsible for this new world of interconnectivity, and frankly, that is the way Xero is built. This experience, although a very painful and expensive two months, ended up being a blessing in disguise, because it eventually led us to the hosted QuickBooks solution in the cloud, and ultimately to Xero. So at the end of the day, what

Xero calls "the Global Xero Ecosystem" turned out to be the Holy Grail for HPC. We will discuss it in detail in a later section.

Zero Entry

For several years, we've been using systems in which customers and vendors can enter accounting data for us when they place orders on our web stores, or when they send us electronic invoices. Compared with the old world of faxes and paper documents (such as sales orders and vendor invoices), in which data were manually entered by the bookkeeper, this is a great leap forward for efficiency, accuracy, and cost reduction in bookkeeping.

The key to zero entry is movement toward connecting business processes with the accounting system via software connections and data flows. We'll realize the goal of zero data entry by connecting customer-entered data, vendor-entered data, employee-entered data, and automated recurring entries that free the bookkeeper from *entering* data. Although we'll never actually reach *zero* entry, the dramatic reduction of data entry from this trend is compelling, and revolutionary.

Collaborative Accounting Services

Accounting professionals also must focus on how to collaborate with clients and serve them in ways that were impossible just a few years ago.

In this new world, cloud computing is the common platform for accountants and clients, where they work collaboratively on the same data at the same time from anywhere in the world. By centralizing the client's data in the cloud (surrounded by robust security measures, both physical and embedded in the network), we can provide clients with the same features and capabilities they used to get from their premise-based systems. But in addition, we can work collaboratively with them and manage their business information.

Examples of products/services:

- Hosted desktop software – Several companies provide desktop software "hosting" whereby Windows servers— loaded with traditional desktop software such as QuickBooks, Microsoft Office, and other business applications—can be accessed via a remote connection over the Internet. This allows accountants and clients to access the same, live data anytime, anywhere.
- Cloud accounting products such as Intacct, QuickBooks Online, Xero, Wave, Kashoo, and others.
- Bill.com, which allows accountants to provide cash management, bill-paying, and/or accounts receivable services.
- Online payroll services such as ZenPayroll, Intuit Online Payroll, SurePayroll, and Payroll Relief all provide online payroll that allow accountants to prepare and manage payroll for clients.

Mobile

Mobile devices have become nearly ubiquitous among business owners, and they allow accountants and clients alike to access data from anywhere. This is an area that is expanding rapidly, as customers, vendors, employees, and managers are increasingly mobile in their jobs.

Perhaps you're wondering why or how mobile devices will impact the bookkeeping and accounting functions. We agree that it may seem like a stretch, but mobile devices are everywhere, and that is already causing businesspeople everywhere to rethink how they can work. For the bookkeeper, there will be apps that will allow the review and recoding of transactions that were "zero-entered," and just need the review step from the bookkeeper. There will be mobile apps for managing workflow, viewing the status of tasks, and even processing payroll. For intense data work, however, we don't think mobile will replace our desktops. We are referring to entering adjusting entries, using spreadsheets, or writing client correspondence. But the vendors will tantalize us with some very useful mobile apps that will help connect us and allow us to remain productive while on the road.

Maybe this scares you, as it did me at first. While it's easy to see the benefits of working on mobile devices, it also presents challenges, or at least risks. First, I'm not sure we really want to have so much access to our work. We already feel guilty when on vacation, if we don't check email or respond to text messages. But I suppose that's up to me to just turn the thing off... But still, expectations of customers, colleagues, and bosses are making that harder to get away with.

Maybe the biggest issue concerning the adoption of mobile devices by accountants is security. If you have all of your clients' data accessible from a mobile phone or tablet, what happens if you lose it? Scary for sure, so there is of course an app for that. Check out www.bikn.com. It's a combination phone app and a key ring that beeps when it gets too far away from your iPhone. It's a great example of how innovators eventually work out a solution to nearly every problem they create.

But beyond just losing the device, the security issues with mobile technology are real, and need better solutions before accountants will embrace it for much real work. So we need to give it time, and remain ever diligent about security.

HPC's and Our Clients' Experience with Mobile
Bruce's Story

Smartphones and tablets have changed the way we do business. If you are like many accountants, you have two or three mobile devices. Or perhaps you are more like me? I have two desktops, one laptop, an iPhone, an iPad, and an eReader, just for myself.

I access my Xero account on my mobile devices using Xero Touch. Xero Touch is the mobile version of Xero. It is available for free in the app store.

Xero Touch makes it simple to reconcile bank and credit card items on a mobile device. Most mornings, I will clear out unreconciled items from the night before, just because it is a simple and satisfying way to start the day. I love the feeling of having no unreconciled items on our Xero dashboard. It is like cleaning out your email inbox each day.

I love being able to see all 500 of my Xero organizations from my phone. I can drill into any client, at any time, and see the status of their Xero account, their cash balances and status of their receivables. It is also really easy to invoice clients on the go.

It doesn't matter whether you are starting on Xero or are a power user, you have access to all of your clients on your mobile device.

There are benefits for our clients as well. Many of our clients spend most of their time in the field. When they finish a job, they can invoice their client immediately without having to return to the office.

And this also influences the behavior of our clients' customers. We have set up their invoices so their customers can click a PayPal link and pay immediately. Some customers pay within minutes of receiving their invoice. Sometimes it has left me wondering how they typed that fast. Now imagine how your clients will feel when they realize that you have helped them invoice and collect their receivables faster. You can see how that is game changer.

*The chief danger in life is that you take
too many precautions.*

Alfred Adler

Chapter 5
Getting over the Fear

Before you can really make the leap to become a cloud-based firm that focuses more on advisory services, you need to fully opt in to taking your firm in that direction. Commit yourself, your staff, and your firm to fundamentally revise your business model. Most likely, you, your staff, and your clients will need to overcome the inevitable fear that comes with making such a big change. And even if you're willing to make the leap, you may have lingering doubts about whether all these cloud-based, accountant-centric tools are anything more than just a passing fad.

To get there, it might help to ask yourself the following question: "What will happen if I don't adopt these new business models?" A recent study by the Oxford Martin School on job losses due to computerization and automation addresses this question in an alarming way. It suggests there's a 94 percent probability that automation will result in job losses for accountants and auditors in the next two decades. The study was summarized in *The Economist* article, "The Onrushing Wave." The data from that study is pretty depressing if you're in the middle of your career as an accountant or auditor. But hang on a minute. That study assumes you won't change your processes and business models to take advantage of the once-in-a-generation changes that are occurring in this second decade of the 21st century. The more important take-away from the study is that the accountants' cheese has moved, and for those who recognize this reality and capitalize on the opportunities, the sky is the limit.

It is finally possible for accountants to deliver what their clients really want as opposed to just serving their compliance needs.

Some History

If you look at history, you'll see many repeated patterns. It's as though we've been here before. *As new innovations come along, there will be many doubters.* So many people focus on why new products won't work, and many struggle to comprehend why the new thing is relevant. Do you remember when you first heard about TiVo? Was it difficult to comprehend what "pausing live TV" even meant? We guess we should only ask that question to people over 40, but you get the point. You can see why people didn't just rush out and empty the shelves of them. They first had to figure out what the thing did, and why they would pay money for it.

Some of the doubters have great reasons to adopt slowly. We've all been burned by one technology or another that showed such promise when we watched the demo, but then didn't work out too well. Such experiences make us take a more conservative, wait-and-see approach to innovation. And perhaps more so than other businesses, accounting cannot afford for its systems to fail in the middle of a busy season. This makes sense on many levels, and it's why accountants have historically been late adopters of new technologies.

Ever since Luca Pacioli published his book *Summa de arithmetica, geometria, proportioni et proportionalità* on double-entry accounting in 1494, the fundamentals of our profession—the essential processes of recording transactions into journals and ledgers—have served us well. Now we might be going out on a limb here, but *we doubt those fundamentals will change anytime soon.*

The pace of technological change, however, is faster than ever, and it's affecting more business models than ever before. So it's worth pausing to consider whether the current trends in technology warrant a dramatic shift in your thinking as to what business you're really in.

If today's changes seem scary, keep in mind that *we've already been through several foundational shifts like this before.* Each shift has created both pain and opportunity. But for sure, those changes could never have been stopped by simply ignoring them or opting out.

For example, in the 1960s and '70s, we had card readers, dumb terminals, and centralized data. Clients recorded transactions in manual journals, and accountants owned the general ledger. Then there was a big shift in the '80s, with the advent of personal computers and accounting programs clients could use in their own offices. Clients got control over the general ledger, and accountants became isolated from client records. In the '00s, we started to see integration—connected services, desktop integration, web connectors—with data still primarily on the desktop, but moving to servers.

Today, the big shift is toward cloud-based software, mobile devices, and remote access to all information. While these trends are not completely new, we have finally reached the adoption tipping point.

In today's business world, the reality for business owners is that *to thrive, they must serve customers online.* Customers expect to interact with every business directly on its website, and through a variety of (increasingly mobile) electronic communication methods. SMBs today must embrace such technologies as e-commerce, web-based customer support, web meetings, web marketing, and collaborative relationships with their customers and suppliers (including their accountant).

All of these require centralized data, and the cloud is the best option for that, whether it's a private cloud, a public cloud, or a hybrid.

The Internet Is the Ultimate Mainframe

A good way to think about the latest trends toward cloud-based, centralized data, accessed via mobile and remote devices, is to imagine a pendulum.

In the mainframe era, the pendulum swung heavily toward centralized data, hardware, and applications. The benefits of mainframes were that we could always rely on a "single source of truth" for data, applications, and even the hardware and system software.

But when the PC revolution came along, it meant "freedom for users," in which everyone could have his or her own data, hardware, and software. This was so attractive because it meant we didn't have to "go to the computer." Instead, we had one of our own. So you can see why PCs took off so successfully, causing the pendulum to swing the other way.

But *the Internet has changed everything.* It has caused the pendulum to return to centralized data and applications, but it keeps the freedom for users because it allows them to access this centralized data from anywhere, on multiple devices. We like to think of the Internet as the ultimate mainframe.

From "Client-Centric" to "Accountant-Centric"

With the PC revolution came software solutions that were "client-centric." These systems put clients in control all of the technology and data they used to run their businesses.

The problem this caused for the accounting profession was that it put distance between the accountant and the data they need to perform their services. The shoe box lived on during the PC revolution, even if the contents of the shoe box often contained digital media. And of course, most of that client-entered data needed extensive cleanup before accountants could produce financial statements or tax returns. So the *client-centric systems caused just as many problems for accountants as they solved for clients.*

Perhaps even more importantly, those client-centric, desktop software products haven't been able to provide businesses with an easy way to do business on the Internet with e-commerce, mobile access, and anytime/anywhere access.

The bottom line is that client-centric desktop accounting systems just did not deliver.

Today, virtually all innovation in the accounting and business-process area for SMBs can be categorized as being collaborative, or even accountant-centric; that is, accountants are in a great position to take advantage of these innovations.

Learning along the Way
Bruce's Story

After returning to Atlanta from Los Angeles in early 2008, I started providing back-office services for a couple of well-established real estate developers. They were great clients. They both had multiple entities (like eight to ten). In real estate, each deal has its own ownership and funding structure, so each deal could involve as many as five legal entities. For you accountants, that means multiple ledgers, tax returns, etc. Not to mention combining or consolidating them.

I knew that business, and taking care of those clients was not difficult for us. As a matter of fact, we paid the bills, did payroll, etc. for one of them. A complete outsourced back office. The only difference was, we had to send one of our bookkeepers to *their* office. Things were humming, the economy was good, real estate was booming. Then each of them ran into issues on their projects. Either the high-rise condos they built weren't selling, or their partners in the deals wouldn't cooperate anymore. In any event, they both declared bankruptcy.

Losing the revenue was bad, and not collecting the receivables was not so good, either. But the worst part was losing almost $200,000 of revenue. That was a material amount to my practice back then. What would you do if you lost more than 25 percent of your business when two clients went away? And we lost others, too. The economy was in the tank, real estate was a bust, and banks weren't lending. (But it's an ill wind that blows no good: I actually gained some valuable experience in helping clients deal with lenders and negotiate short-sales, forbearance agreements, and deeds in lieu.) In the end, however, I needed to find something else. Bring on technology and let's build a recurring revenue practice with new tools.

More Opportunities for Accountants

As an accounting professional, your success lies in thinking through your strategies for how you can leverage these new trends in technology, and how you can position yourself and your firm to become change leaders for your clients. Clients are seeking this type of advisor, one who knows how to take advantage of new opportunities.

Change Leadership

The world is full of theories on change management; but we submit that people simply don't want to be managed. Rather, they're desperate for leadership. If you put yourself out as a change leader—one who understands your clients' businesses perhaps even better than they do—they'll follow your leadership. But this will require you to completely opt in. It will require that you dig much deeper into each client's business and bring all your technical and accounting knowledge to the table. This kind of commitment takes many accountants out of their comfort zone, but if you're committed to growing your practice, the best way to accomplish this is to start *leading* your clients, instead of simply *serving* their compliance needs.

As this new world takes shape, it will allow small businesses to work collaboratively with their accountants. The cloud-based, centralized data methods allow accountants to do more of what they do well, while simultaneously allowing business owners and bookkeepers to focus less on accounting and more on growing the business.

Leadership comes only when you're willing to do things that customers are not completely familiar with. Eventually, they *will* ask about what others are doing. But the inspired accountant anticipates the clients' needs and finds solutions *before* they ask.

*Decide that you want it more than you
are afraid of it.*

Bill Cosby

Chapter 6
Believing the Value

One of the hardest things we had to deal with was believing the value. If we didn't think our work was worth more than the billing rate, how could we expect our clients to? When your typical bookkeeping client pays you $375 a month, how can you expect them to pay you $750, or better yet, $1,500? The key is to actually provide them with more than just bookkeeping. Many a client appreciates the peace of mind they gain from knowing that a team of professionals has their back. Others are willing to pay a premium for having a (most trusted) advisor when they have to make tough business decisions. All of these things are now on the table, due to updated financial information being available 24/7 from the cloud.

Xero has been the centerpiece of HPC being able to provide the value. The real-time data, and all the things that come along with it, allow us to work closer with our clients. But it all begins with learning how to use the tool and believing in it.

A big part of believing the value is valuing your own time, and you will know that you're doing that when you find yourself willing to say "buh-bye" to a client. For the longest time, I, Bruce, never fired a client; under the old paradigm, it just didn't happen. But at some point I started listening to others who had done this. They talked about how good it felt, the reduced stress and, of course, being able to do other things, whether they were work-related or not.

One of the biggest mistakes a company can make is keeping a client that doesn't fit their business model. And when you think about it, keeping those clients does them just as big a disservice as you're doing to yourself. If you are not seriously looking at your client list at least once a year, you are probably carrying clients that you shouldn't be. Some say you should fire your bottom 20 percent each year.

There are as many reasons to fire a client as there are clients, but here are eight red flags that we keep our eyes peeled for.

1. Not appreciating the service you provide, or the effort that goes into serving them

2. Being unreachable or unwilling to return your calls

3. A tendency to procrastinate, which results in emergencies for your firm

4. Being disrespectful in any way

5. A belief that everything should be easy or quick

6. An inability to be satisfied no matter what you do

7. An unwillingness to do what is necessary so that you can serve them

8. Constantly complaining about fees, or worse, not paying you

Things are always changing, especially when it comes to technology. A good business will always try to adapt to changing circumstances, which sometimes means changing the business model. Remember that when you begin to find too much comfort in the thought of the revenue you are earning from a large legacy business; in the end, it will cost you. You'll find that situations like that eat away at your core competencies, not to mention your valuable time. We all know it, yet we find accepting it so terribly difficult.

What can you do it about it? Create a policy to review your client list at least once a year, maybe even twice a year. You know who they are. You most likely don't even need a list or system. You know it in your gut.

Think about all the pain that could be avoided by firing such a client. For example:

- A dispute snowballing into a lawsuit
- The risk that they could run off a key staff member
- The sheer stress of simply dealing with them

The best advice we can give is to follow your instincts. In the end, they are almost always correct.

Being the most trusted advisor has its advantages. Clients want your advice; you just have to be willing to provide it. If you do provide it, you are adding value to your service, and they will be willing to pay for it. A perfect example is our first big full-service back-office client. We estimated a fixed monthly fee of $5,000. We had never had a monthly client who was serviced through the cloud for anywhere near that amount. But after explaining to them how this would actually save them money, and spare them the bother of having to replace and retrain an in-house accountant when their current one leaves (as they inevitably do), they were sold.

We spelled out the savings to them, along with the many other benefits of working with us, and they loved it. They had gone through some turnover in their staff, and the people they had in their accounting department did not have the expertise that we could provide. So they could upgrade their knowledge level, have an accounting team instead of just an accountant, and be rid of the worries concerning the departure of their current accountant and training a new one. All that was now our problem, and we were saving them money. Laid out like that, it was a no-brainer.

The difference between successful people and very successful people is that very successful people say "no" to almost everything.

Warren Buffett

Chapter 7
Specialize for
Success

Should Accountants Specialize?

The percentage of SMBs who require or prefer their CPA to be a specialist in their industry increased from 53 percent in 2013 to 62 percent in 2014 (Figure 2). This may indicate a growing desire among SMBs for CPAs with knowledge of technological solutions for specific industries. There's still a significant number of SMBs who don't care if their CPA is a specialist, and a possible reason for this is the misconception there's no need for industry expertise unless the accountant is helping them with business planning, technology planning, or business-process engineering. This could be a strong warning sign that SMBs who answered "don't care" are only receiving compliance services (e.g., tax preparation and financial statements), which is quickly becoming a commoditized service. In the coming years, the real opportunities for accounting professionals will be in advisory services, which drive deeper relationships with clients.

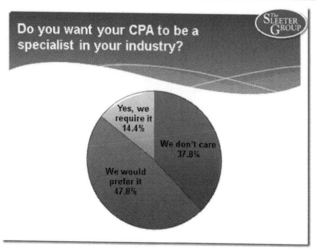

Figure 2 Specialize for Success

Specialization at HPC
Bruce's Story

While I believe specialization is definitely the way to go, we didn't start out that way. At first, we were just looking for Xero clients, with whom we could learn this new way of bookkeeping. I was willing to take on just about anyone, not necessarily because I thought we would end up keeping all these clients, but to learn—and learn we did. Many of our clients from that time were clearly not a good fit for HPC, but we didn't know that yet. The fit was off for different reasons. With some, there was a disconnect around technological expertise, others didn't have the internal resources to own the parts of the relationship that we needed them to own.

One of these clients was a nonprofit organization. I had some experience with nonprofits, and knew some things about fund accounting, but our staff really did not. We struggled, and finally realized we should stick to what we all know. So I would say to clients, find an accounting firm that really knows how to take care of you. The good news was, we had a legacy practice that still had some cash flow; we weren't desperate and could experiment a little. And over time, we learned to identify clients that fit well with us, and what were the characteristics of a good Xero client.

In those early days, I thought that being the entire the back office was the way to go, partly because of the situation one of our first clients was in. They were a mess when we began our work for them, so doing the entire back office kind of made sense. But at the time, we didn't have the processes in place to property identify just how messy the situation really was. It took a long time to clean things up and get into a routine. But hey, we were very patient, we did things right, and I am proud to say that they are still a valuable client. But if I knew then what I do now, I would have embraced that engagement totally another way.

As we scanned the horizon for more Xero clients, we learned to be more critical about the types of transactions different companies make, and what their accounting needs really were. The needs of a start-up technology company are different from an e-commerce retailer. A law firm is different from a real estate management company. A restaurant different from a consulting company.

As we learned how to identify good Xero clients, we also got up to speed on important characteristics of specific vertical markets. There is no question that specialized industry knowledge makes a difference. Of course it matters in providing service, but it also matters in the sales process. Specialized knowledge always helps to close the deal. Even if you are not providing higher-level advisory services, but you are providing the valuable bookkeeping services, industry knowledge still allows you to be more valuable to your client and more efficient in the bookkeeping. Being more valuable to the client encourages the client to become stickier, and efficiency means more profit for you.

Our strengths were with technology companies, start-ups, venture capital, and private equity. We understood what they needed, and our team had industry experience. Our model started with trying to do a little of everything. And our business blossomed once we focused on our core strengths.

We were approached in early 2013 by an Australian client. This forward-thinking company did their books in Xero and wanted to enter the US market. With our company's specialty in taxes, we helped them form their first US legal entity. We saw the opportunity and began to focus on other global companies using Xero and entering the US market. . Now, a week doesn't go by when another international business isn't contacting us asking if we can help them. By specializing, we are not only growing as a company, but I have the satisfaction of knowing that we have clients on six continents around the world.

Over time, we not only realized what we were good at, but also what type of clients we enjoyed working with. As we added more clients in our favorite verticals, we began to generate a virtuous circle, in which our specialized expertise attracted clients who needed that expertise. Clients want accountants and CPAs who can provide solutions to their challenges. They will hire you, and pay you nicely, for that experience.

You can do anything, but not everything.

David Allen

Chapter 8
Agility Trumps Ability

In the new world of chunkified business processes, there will most certainly be no single solution, or standard set of solutions that will do all things for all clients. Chunkification allows us to stop force-fitting and begin tailoring a best-of-breed solution at each step of each business process for each client.

The pace of change is faster than ever, which means that accountants who focus more on agility than on raw ability will thrive in the coming years. Technical skills and knowledge are table stakes, admittedly, but those skills won't be enough in the new world unless you also develop the ability to use a variety of technologies to apply your skills.

Those who insist on sticking to the old-paradigm processes and business models will find it very difficult to compete in an accounting services marketplace where more agile, entrepreneurial, and skilled professionals are building successful firms that provide services more tailored to what SMBs want.

Choose Agility
Bruce's Story

Once I decided to embrace the new paradigm, I went to all the accounting conferences that were oriented that way, and learned as much as I could about what was out there. At the same time, I reached out to the thought leaders in our industry to pick their brains. All this was as much to validate what I was committed to as it was to learn new things. I looked at each of the vendors in the cloud space and tried to pick what appeared to be, in the Gartner Group's parlance, the best of breed. And after I identified them, the next step was to figure out how to make them all talk with each other. I did that by contacting the vendors, whose systems addressed key functions in our business, and then I lobbied—in some cases, you could say harassed—them to work together.

The first one we selected was SmartVault, and they were going to take us paperless as our vehicle for an electronic filing cabinet. Here's how all that unfolded.

Back when I was in Los Angeles working with the digital media industry, HPC made the decision to move to a Thomson virtual office product. While it was really good product, it definitely wasn't going to talk to any other software that we might have selected in the future. That decision was probably a good decision at the time, but wasn't a good decision considering the future we were headed for. It was a Holy Grail kind of product. Thomson wanted all of their clients on their suite of products. So when it came time to embrace cloud technology, since we were already one of their products, Thomson Virtual Office was the path of least resistance. I already told you about what a disaster that was, and what we learned from it. My take-away was that cloud technology was the future, and there were tons of advantages for us with it. We just picked the wrong horse out of the gate.

At that time, I made it my mission to rid HPC of all our servers. There is almost nothing worse than spending money each month on maintaining a crumbling infrastructure. Yet most small firms don't have the expertise or resources to do it in-house. So you are at the mercy of your IT consultant/provider, who you really want to be thinking outside the box when it comes to file servers, exchange servers, etc.

So much for hardware, what about software? When Microsoft announced they weren't going support XP anymore, we reached another decision point. It wasn't so much of a turning point, as that it just proved our point. The cloud was the way to go, and we were going to embrace it.

I am proud to say that, after about three years, our servers are now *gone*. All our software is as-a-service, and 100 percent in the cloud. The one product that we hung onto until going completely into the cloud was our time and billing system, Office Tools Professional. It was a great product, I really liked it, but the problem was it wasn't in the cloud. When we started using virtual workers, they had to dial into our office computers just to report their time. Plus, it didn't give us the real-time, shared project management that we knew we had to have to scale and grow. When we finally made the decision to migrate to AffinityLive, the servers were decommissioned.

We also reclaimed the space we had dedicated to our file room. By now, we have been on SmartVault long enough that we not only have had a server-bashing celebration, but also a shredding party. All of our old paper files have been either scanned or shredded, and we no longer need our file room.

Taking a cue from some of our high-tech and hip clients, I decided to make it over into a lounge room. We are now in the process of cleaning out the file room racks, and will soon replace them with couches and a ping-pong table. Not too bad for a traditional CPA for more than twenty years.

The moral of the story here is, don't be afraid to try new things. Educate yourself so you know what options are available. Then experiment. You won't succeed on everything, and every decision will not be the right one. But at least you can avoid some of the pitfalls that have claimed other victims. Be agile, and you will succeed too.

Creation is in part merely the business of forgoing the great and small distractions.

E.B. White

Chapter 9
There's an App for that, too: Xero's Developer Ecosystem

Ecosystems Beget Product Success

When selecting software in today's chunkified world, it's critically important that you consider the ecosystem of developer add-ons that connect and add value to the software you're purchasing. Examples of how add-ons contribute value are everywhere. Photoshop would never be the powerhouse it is without the rich developer ecosystem that has created those crucial and sometimes obscure add-on features (that they call plug-ins) that so many users could not live without. For many users, the add-ons make all the difference, and they would go with a different image editor if it provided the add-ons.

Similarly for cloud accounting software: add-ons are critical. Since most cloud accounting software products, Xero included, don't provide as many core business process functions as you found with desktop accounting systems in the old paradigm, the successful implementation of Xero requires users to find the add-ons that meet their needs.

What Ecosystems Must Have

At the core of a successful developer ecosystem is a robust means for developers to "get under the hood," or, in developers' parlance, an application programming interface (API). To understand how APIs work, consider two separate programs. We'll call them "Accounting" and "Payroll." For this discussion, Payroll is an add-on to Accounting.

In order for Payroll to work with Accounting, the Accounting developer must create an API, which consists of program libraries and interfaces that Payroll developers will use to access the Accounting database and exchange data there. The Payroll application will need to both read and write data into Accounting, so the API needs to have sufficient power to facilitate reading, writing, and updating data in Accounting.

Each software ecosystem needs APIs that are robust enough to support the type of integrations that a variety of add-ons will need. If an API doesn't have enough features, add-on developers won't come because they cannot access the data necessary to create a successful product in the marketplace.

Beyond the API, the Accounting system must also provide support programs, marketing programs, and partnering programs that help the add-on developers like Payroll build their business and capture as many of the Accounting users as possible.

APIs and marketing and support for developers are critical drivers of success for all applications, and especially in the SMB accounting marketplace.

Bruce's Thoughts on Xero's Developer Ecosystem
Bruce's Story

When considering whether to adopt Xero in your practice or recommend it to your clients, don't consider just Xero alone. Be sure to include the developer ecosystem. In my opinion, creative developers will always show up whenever, in any SMB vertical, some accountant begins to scratch his head and say, "there must be an app for this." If you limit yourself to just Xero, you may wind up thinking that Xero doesn't have a feature you need. But I would argue that you shouldn't expect any software to do everything for everybody. Instead, look for a *collection of solutions* that can accomplish what you need.

This isn't to say that many SMBs need a solution such as Intacct or NetSuite, which offer more in their accounting software than a Xero, QBO, or QBD can provide. Intacct and NetSuite are excellent cloud options, and if they fit the bill for you, that's great.

But with the advent of true SaaS, or cloud-based software that was created to be distributed and used over the Internet, fewer firms will find a monolithic solution that will do everything for them. Xero was designed from the ground up with an open API infrastructure that facilitates the development of add-ons that seamlessly interact with Xero's databases. Basically, once the connection is made, you're done. There are no exports and imports, formatting, or pushing buttons. Because of this, Xero has attracted more than 350 add-on partners who have built some pretty neat tools for SMBs. Each one of these add-ons were designed to fill a void or fit a need experienced by different types of businesses. Their capabilities range across bills and expenses, CRM, e-commerce, inventory, point of sale, payroll and HR, time tracking, payments, and reporting. To me, this is what chunkification really means.

Because of our position as Xero's leading partner, a week doesn't go by that I don't hear from some software company that wants to either work with us, work for us, or have us test their software. These companies could be from anywhere, and that's the thing about this Xero ecosystem, it is truly global. It was not easy for Xero to make the shift from being an unknown New Zealand-based software company to crack into the U.S. market (just ask Rod Drury), but thanks to this global view, it seems to be happening. Companies like Spotlight, Fathom, AffinityLive, and ReceiptBank see the huge market potential in the U.S., and find it just too good to pass up. Many of these developers were already connected to QuickBooks.

So how does this affect you? How about making it easier to create workflow solutions and efficiencies for your clients? How about enabling *your* firm to work more effectively and efficiently? HPC recently did an inventory of all of our clients and the Xero add-on partners they use. I was shocked to see that they were using almost fifty add-ons. Granted, we don't use or support that many. But our clients do, and they are using them effectively in their businesses.

Our next mission is figure out how many add-ons the average Xero client is using. My guess is that we are going to see a number in the three to five range. The best part for us is that we can have several truly integrated workflow solutions for different kinds of businesses, so when clients or prospects finally ask us, we can basically offer them their back office in a box (which is in the shape of a cloud). For some that may be

Xero, ZenPayroll, Bill.com, and Expensify. For others it may be Xero, ADP, Shopify, StitchLabs, and ReceiptBank. The point is, there are tools available for just about every specific need, and they are relatively easy for us to piece together (thanks to the ecosystem approach). What's more, there are advisors who are excellent at testing and reviewing the add-ons for each function, complete with feature comparisons and limitations. Many in the Xero Community love to share their knowledge, just like we are doing here.

It's not the load that breaks you down,
it's the way you carry it.

Lena Horne

Chapter 10
A Few Bumps along the Road to Success

The most important issues in building a successful cloud-based practice come down to three things: product, people, and process. Regarding product, as you can see from the title of this book, my practice has opted in for Xero. For CRM and project management, though, we use AffinityLive.

Note: The first-person examples used throughout this chapter are from Bruce Phillips.

Experience with Tools (Product)

While Xero may not be for everyone, it has worked for HPC —although for some very specific reasons. What benefits has Xero brought to my practice? Let's break them down into categories and talk about each one.

- Ease of access
- Security
- Cost
- Real-time financial information
- Ability to work from anywhere

- Flexibility and scalability
- An environment that promotes collaboration among staff and with clients

Ease of Access

With Xero, you can access your clients' data from anywhere, on any device connected to the Internet, and at any time. As it is SaaS, there's no need to install software on any device, and it updates automatically. As a matter of fact, Xero updates its software every three weeks. The beauty of that is that *you don't have to do anything.* In the event of a natural disaster, fire, or even catastrophic weather (such as we had in Atlanta in January 2014), you have nothing to worry about. No downtime, in either the software or your workflow. As long as you have power and access to the Internet, you're in business. In addition, Xero features specific access controls, so you can define the areas that your users can get into. All this eliminates an awful lot of emailing, and you will never again have to swap disks or use flash drives.

Security

Responsible cloud-based companies know that world-class security is a top priority. There's no way your firm could secure its servers and desktops to the level that Xero secures its data centers. Xero has redundant servers in multiple locations that are secured physically through identity management, and technologically by multilayered firewalls and hardened intrusion-protection systems. In the event your laptop is stolen, gets lost, or simply crashes, no worries; your clients' data remains safe and unaffected.

Cost

Using Xero involves virtually no capital expenditure (except for the computers and/or mobile devices that you use to access it). Xero also has a policy of allowing an unlimited number of users access to any licensee's account (with the security measures just mentioned); you pay only by company. Similarly with clients, they pay only one license fee per entity. Currently, those fees range from $9 to $30 per month, unless you need multicurrency or you're using it for payroll with more than one employee. Accountants get their Xero Partner practice account for free. So there really is no reason not to try it.

Real-time Financial Information

Xero's bank and credit cards feeds are the reason most accountants find Xero so effective (never mind the awesome user interface). There's nothing like waking up every day and logging in to your Xero accounts, and seeing all of the transactions just sitting there waiting for some love (review and reconciliation). Many of our clients reconcile every day. Forget about closing the books at the end of the month. I get my monthly financial statements on the first of the month, and can see exactly where I am any day during the month. The feeds are great, but would be nothing without Xero's Bank Rules and Cash Coding. *Bank Rules* make is easy to reconcile by using a multifaceted logic, and *Cash Coding* has become our best friend. Only available to financial advisors in Xero, *Cash Coding* makes it possible in many instances to reconcile thousands of transactions in just an hour or two.

I know that other software may have similar features. But the way Xero does it improves workflow from our perspective. It is not just about the bank feeds, bank rules, and cash coding. It's the gamification of it, color coding, side-by-side presentation, and nomenclature. It is the way everything comes together.

Ability to Work from Anywhere

When I travel, I like to have access to all of my clients' data. Do you think my clients appreciate the fact that I can see their data anytime from anywhere when they have a question? You bet they do. Do I add value by being accessible? I sure do. Are they willing to pay for that? They sure are. But the best part for me is that I like to travel. Now I can do that as much as I want. I even have found that I do some of my best work on cruise ships in the middle of the ocean.

Flexibility and Scalability

As you grow your business and add staff, there's no additional cost for additional users, the way there is in most environments. There also are no time-consuming installations and upgrades (other than providing a computer or laptop). Xero has multiple pricing plans for both its Business edition and Partner edition. We use the Partner edition for small clients and for what accountants call "write-up."

Collaboration among Staff

The way HPC's business model has evolved, we typically assign several employees to each client's account. As I write these words, they happen to be in Georgia, Wisconsin, and California. They can all can log into the same client's account, and work with the same data, at the same time. This allows us to be extremely efficient with our staffing and managing our costs.

Collaborative Consulting with Clients

Although all the other points I've mentioned above are important, I left this one for last, because this it is the reason why we do what we do. Under the old paradigm, we had to wait for files, disks, or for the client to do something. In this new Xero world, we can use real-time data and advise our clients in real time. We have timely information to help our clients make timely business decisions. We have taken control of the client relationship. This is how we solidify our position as the most trusted advisor. This is how we add value.

These are all excellent reasons why Xero has worked so well for HPC. But in addition to all of the above, there's yet another benefit—a monetary one. Because of what we've done and how we've adopted Xero and the Xero ecosystem, we now serve our clients better with fewer staff, hence improving *our* bottom line.

Eventually, just about everyone asks: "How do I get started?"

If you're a CPA, an accountant, a CFO, an enrolled agent, or anything similar, what you need to do is set yourself up on Xero. It's easy. It's free. And you don't need to stop tracking your revenue and expenses however you're currently doing it. Just set up a free trial Xero account, import your chart of accounts, and connect your bank accounts and credit card (if you have one). You can keep a cash set of books, play with Xero, and see for yourself how easy it really is. Of course, you can use other features too, but you don't have to.

What you'll find is that with Xero's bank feeds, bank rules, and cash coding, you can produce monthly profit-and-loss reports very easily. If you're adventurous, you can even invoice your clients and see the power of matching. You don't have to actually send these invoices to clients. Continue to use whatever system you're currently using for that (at least until you make a decision). If you don't find it amazing and fun (I actually find it fun), I will be shocked. It's like playing a game of Tetris—*really!* And I am not the only one saying this. I have heard it from many clients, and even from other thought leaders who run their businesses on Xero.

As far as ease, once I felt comfortable with it, I turned everything over to a non-accountant to manage. Yes, a non-accountant. You don't need to understand debits and credits, because Xero uses terms like "Spend Money" and "Receive Money." If you don't understand spending and receiving money, then we probably need to have a more elementary conversation.

Well, with what Xero has accomplished for HPC in the past two years, I can give you $200 million reasons Xero is here to stay. Seriously, while fundraising and investors definitely help, the strides Xero has made with the product, the fact that it was built specifically for the cloud, and how its global ecosystem has taken off and flourished have convinced us that we picked the right horse in this race.

Experience with Staff (People)

The second issue is people. And the first thing about people is that, in order to either start your Xero practice, you *must* have a Xero champion. This person has to be a leader, and it is always better if this person is a partner or principal, and for the champion to have experience in consulting or operational accounting.

Any substantive change in your firm requires someone who will own that change. I have spoken with many firms of all sizes, and one thing that he discovered is that every firm that successfully implemented Xero had a champion for in the office. When you are trying to effect change, no matter what the change is, you need an individual who will continually challenge the status quo. Otherwise, the change stalls. Of course every firm is different in terms of size, number of partners, departments, staff, etc. The larger the organization, the more important it is to have a Xero champion, and the champion must have the unflinching support of firm leadership. Ideally, the Xero champion *will be* firm leadership. With HPC, that was the case.

Another essential in changing the direction of your firm, such as when implementing Xero, is education and training. Education and training means something different to everybody. In HPC's case, Xero came on-site and gave a one-day session. While it wasn't very effective at the time, it did serve a purpose. It became obvious throughout the exercise who was going to be *in*, and who was not. While certain staff learned the new software and the new ways of doing everything, others never really embraced Xero. To move the needle and learn the ways, you have to use it every day. Bottom line: use it or lose it. By the time this book is published, those who didn't get on the bus and embrace Xero will no longer be part of HPC.

A third critical component of making a successful change is your staff. They *must* have certain skills, such as:

- Technological proficiency
- Excellent communication skills
- Ability to accept constant change
- The right personality
- A love of learning

All of these are vitally important to your practice. As a matter of fact, we turned our staff over twice while we were building our Xero practice. I cannot emphasize enough the importance of having the right people. It makes all the difference in the world. The thing that was so amazing to me, was that I didn't know what I didn't have, until I had it. Looking back, we had the wrong staff in nearly every position, and that was my fault. I let the culture become one in which less-than-perfection was acceptable. We had no accountability. Now, I can't imagine the time that I couldn't totally rely and trust my team. We truly have the best team ever. Everyone knows their role and takes responsibility for what they do. And most importantly, each team member is the best at what they do and they hold each other accountable.

Anyone who has heard me speak has heard the bit about my favorite part of the week: Wednesday at 1:00pm Eastern Time. That is when we have our weekly staff video call. We talk about everything that is going on in the practice, and cut up a little. Each person has a few minutes to discuss what they are doing, what resources they need, and what they have to share with the other departments. Because so many of us work at home, attire isn't an issue. My only requirement is that I want to see each person's face once a week. So team, I don't care what you do, you will be on with video. We have seen hats, muscle shirts, and you name it. But we get a lot accomplished and have a lot of fun doing it.

Experience with Workflow (Process)

Last but equally important, is the process. For without process you cannot scale. And without scaling, you cannot grow. And if you are not growing, you are in trouble.

Let's start with my favorite process, sales. I wasn't always a good sales person. And if you remember when I was talking about Tony Halligan hiring me, at that point I had never sold anything. To sell you need to believe more than sell. For me, the experience is mostly listening to what the prospect wants and needs, and then explaining to him or her how we work. I believe that, for many potential clients, we have the best product, people, and processes. So when I talk about it, my belief becomes evident. Prospects and clients recognize and are attracted to confidence. Your confidence allows them to have confidence in you. Confidence makes closing the right clients a breeze.

We strive to break down each interaction with every prospect to make sure that working with us is easy for them. This begins with our first email or phone call. We design each touch to give them the best experience. Once we decide that we want to work with a particular client, we make sure that we understand their scope and how to set our fee. After we agree on that, we move to engagement letter, always keeping the client's ease and comfort with the process in mind. After they sign up (using electronic signature that they can do on their iPad or mobile device), we move to document gathering and getting them set up in our systems. We have worked tirelessly to perfect our project plans and workflow. Our process for serving clients can be broken down to the following:

- Finding and choosing
- Onboarding and implementing
- Maintaining

Process accounts for nothing without the right tools, which we mostly covered earlier in the Product section. Obviously, we chose Xero. But we also chose AffinityLive, an Australia-based CRM and project management solution that is part of the Xero ecosystem that we chose for several reasons. One of which was functionality. But we also knew that we needed our CRM system to grow, even though we had never used one before. We also needed time, billing, and other features such as support tickets, and email campaigns. AffinityLive gives us all of that in one package. We create invoices in AffinityLive and access them in Xero, where they are ready to edit and send to clients.

We figured it would take a couple cycles to learn how best to use it for our advantage. We focused first on accounting projects, and then put it through its paces on tax projects. After a few months, it became apparent that at least the project management part was going to be a very good fit. I love the color-coded dashboards for different project types, which allow us to monitor the status of each project. We have time budgets and tasks, and now have templates customized to practically every function and process for each type of project that we do. Individuals in the office have project-type responsibilities to make sure that each project gets set up correctly and progresses to a satisfactory completion.

We have our project types segregated like this:

- Accounting-recurring
  - Support

- Bookkeeping
- Advisory

* Accounting-nonrecurring
    - Special projects
    - Set up and conversions
* Tax
    - Recurring
    - Special projects

This allows us to track each project in terms of tasks, costs, and revenue. It even allows us to project revenue and monitor our run rate. Although we provide professional services, I learned early on that recurring revenue and run rate are *key*. All of our software clients track it. Why shouldn't we? Recurring revenue helps pay the bills. I can't tell you how good if feels when the clients' monthly payments hit on the first of each month. Ideally, if you can get your recurring monthly revenue to cover all of your expenses, you are golden! That should be your goal. The Xero model has made it possible for us.

Overall, we are still tweaking our use of AffinityLive, but it is always good to strive to do things better and more efficiently. The templates really simplified the process of monitoring what has been done versus not been done. More importantly, the system prevents us from letting steps fall through the cracks.

All of our service offerings also come down to process. After many iterations, we finally settled on three types of basic accounting services, or processes: support, bookkeeping, and advisory. We have broken down each one very specifically. We know each action and notification that is necessary. For example, our support service includes client contact each month that we review their Xero account. We also provide a monthly review of their bank and credit card statements and activity to ensure they stay in balance. Our bookkeeping process involves reconciliations, review, financial reports, and regular communication. Advisory involves more controllership and CFO functions. We have detailed processes for each service, and we create each of these processes from a template. AffinityLive was not intended to track time, but we set it up to do so; that way, we can see how we are doing.

All of this boils to down to what I call "the experience." Your clients will stay with you if you provide them with the best experience possible. And to do that, you need the best product, the best people, and the best processes. If you make it easy to work with your firm, clients will come, and stay.

People, Processes, and Products at HPC
Bruce's Story

So now you know a bit of our history, the mistakes we made, and the lessons we learned along the way. Our most recent turning point came gradually, from February to December, 2013. That is when Ann, Jen, and Sharon joined HPC.

Now we have a person with great skills in project management, organization, and communication for onboarding, converting, clean-up, and training. We also have the right person with CFO and advisory skills that provides proactive advice in everyday language to our clients. And we have the right person with client service and support skills, someone who is highly organized and a great communicator.

The only problem, as I saw it at first, was that just one of them was actually in Atlanta. At the time, I still thought that I needed to lay eyes on each member of the team every day. Otherwise, how could I evaluate how well we were communicating, how tightly we were bonding, and—especially—how hard they were working? Boy, was that ever a wrong-headed idea! Soon enough, I simply saw how effective each one was at what she was doing, and realized that where they actually were wasn't such an important issue after all. When you have the right people working with the right tools, and they all are carrying out documented, repeatable, and reportable processes, you will find that your efforts become even more valuable than ever, regardless of whether your team is geographically concentrated or dispersed.

Even with the right people and most of the right tools, however, we still needed tighter integration for our communications and a better system for project management. I was leaning heavily toward WorkflowMax to fill the project management and CRM holes. With the entire firm oriented around Xero (internally and externally, except for a few legacy clients), and Xero having just bought WorkflowMax, it just seemed like a no-brainer. But try as I might, I just couldn't get it to do the things we needed done. Plus, its interface had what appeared to me as an antiquated look and feel (although Xero was promising that a new skin in development would give the system the same look and feel as Xero, which was in fact finished just prior to the publication of this book. I haven't yet looked closely enough to know if it would work for us now).

So we went on a three-month hunting expedition, in which we evaluated all the CRM and project management software that could function in the Xero ecosystem. After narrowing our choices down to three, we finally selected AffinityLive, and have been delighted with our choice. Geoff McQueen and his team did whatever had to be done to get the system integrated into our Xero environment. Now we can easily track our projects by type and department, our delegated tasks, and our sales pipeline (up to this point, I had been using my iPhone's notes app for pipeline reports). And everyone loves its intuitive, color-coded dashboards.

Remember when I was talking about ditching our servers? The upshot of that episode was using a hosted exchange at AppRiver. At that time, email was practically our only means of communication, although Skype's voice, video, and IM chat capabilities came in handy when I was traveling abroad. Eventually, we started using GoToMeeting for screen sharing, but couldn't integrate it into the Xero ecosystem as tightly as we wanted to. So we looked into Microsoft Lync, which is a very affordable, corporate-oriented IM client that also has voice and video conferencing capabilities, and screen sharing.

In January 2014, we decided to go with AffinityLive and Microsoft Lync. Now, every member of the team can communicate via chat, voice, video, and screen sharing with every other member, with the ecosystem integrating every aspect of our communications. Collaboration was never this tight, even when we all worked at the same address. AffinityLive and Lync were the last two pieces of our puzzle— at least until we decide to tackle a more complicated puzzle.

The measure of our intelligence is our ability to change.

Albert Einstein

Chapter 11
Making It Happen
In Your Practice

However fascinating you find the history of HPC and our experience in embracing the new paradigm of providing the additional value available through cloud-based services, it will remain just another story you've heard unless you make the decision to make that move yourself. To help you with that, here's a ten-step program for familiarizing yourself with Xero and using it as a base for transforming your practice.

Note: The first-person examples used throughout this chapter are from Bruce.

1: Go Paperless

OK. You are probably never going to get to a completely paperless practice, but the point here is to understand the inefficiencies of paper, as opposed to digital databases, as a recording medium. Transferring information from one piece of paper to another is slow and prone to errors. Transferring information from one database to another is instantaneous and error free. So until you have dramatically reduced the amount of paper your practice uses, less paper will always be better.

Going paperless improves workflow because the transfer of digital information is immediate. Take the example of individual tax return files. Scanning them as soon as possible, and having all that information available electronically means that anyone can work with that information at any time from any place with an Internet connection. Having that information available electronically also means that you can use it in other contexts. That is, it is flexible. In addition, the greater efficiency of a paperless practice allows you to scale up your operations, which enables greater productivity.

The portable document format (PDF), developed by Adobe Systems in the early 1990s, enables electronic documents to be created, shared, and edited, regardless of application software, hardware, and operating systems. PDFs offer greater security than documents created in any typical word-processing program, which makes them ideal for marking, ticking, and modifying work papers. Since the format was first developed, dozens of tools have arrived on the scene that help you accomplish all the tasks you would normally do with paper documents. It doesn't take long to discover the ones that will be most useful for you. So identify them, evaluate them, make a short list, and make your choice(s). Develop a plan for converting your paper to PDFs, and enjoy the benefits of having carried it out.

2. Get Rid of Your Internal Servers

In the old world, servers were an absolute necessity. Nearly every business on the planet had to build internal IT infrastructure to handle core functions such as email hosting, database services, file sharing, internal process documentation, and other corporate data. But the new world is full of robust alternatives that were not possible until a few years ago. Many of the core functions that were only available from inside-the-firewall windows servers, are now possible by cloud solutions, but even those functions you decide to keep in the Windows environment can be moved to a cloud hosting provider such as Cloud9 Real Time, InsynQ, Xcentric, UniData, Right Networks and others. These companies have secure data centers with the highest quality hardware, networking, and security available. These companies allow you to create a virtual server, accessible via the Internet. You can have as much RAM and disk as you need, and you can load pretty much any software you want as long as you ask for a "dedicated" virtual server. Some software might not work, so check with the providers before jumping in, but it's our experience everything you're likely to need can be hosted at one or more of the providers out there.

Moving away from internal servers to hosted servers means you no longer have to invest in local hardware and IT support to keep your internal servers running. Instead, you just log into the remote server where all the applications and data are available 24/7 from anywhere. And the hosting provider handles all of the support, maintenance, security, and backups for your servers. For more on this topic, read Doug's blog post and the discussion following at http://www.sleeter.com/blog/?p=5608.

3. Get Started with Xero

Now, you should be ready to get started with Xero. It is free to try for accountants, and Xero provides all the support you need to get started. So you really have nothing to lose, as you'll be getting a valuable education even if you don't stay with it. A good way to explore its capabilities and gain competency is to set up your practice, creating your chart of accounts and hooking up your banks and credit cards. Set up bank rules and see how everything works and looks. Give yourself as much time as you need before offering Xero service to any clients. My guess is that you will love it if you try it.

During this time, break down all your workflows into specific tasks. This will give you an advantageous perspective on what really is involved in your invoicing, your accounts payable, your payroll, and so on. That perspective will come in handy when you begin perusing the Xero ecosystem for workflow tools. There are hundreds of them, so it will take a little time to evaluate them, but chances are you will find exactly what you need. We found that Bill.com and ZenPayroll were good places to start. You will see how easy these add-ons are to integrate into your Xero system.

Once you've convinced yourself that Xero is the way you want to go, and feel that your comfort level in using it is sufficient for your actual practice, the time to begin migrating selected clients of your practice has come. There is more advice below on how to do that.

4. Evaluate and Educate Your Staff

There is no harm in repeating myself again: Using Xero in your practice can fundamentally change the way you do business. Its basic advantage is that it facilitates the move from being a shop full of compliance technicians to becoming your clients' most trusted advisor. Bookkeeping will no longer be a once-a-month or once-a-quarter chore; Xero enables you to do it on whatever schedule makes sense for each client—even daily or on-demand. You're always working with real-time data, so there is no waiting for files or bank statements to arrive.

Naturally, all this means that your staff must be ready and willing to embrace the new paradigm. Begin by educating them about the advantages the firm will gain by providing valuable advisory services to your clients, and introduce Xero as the vehicle that you all will drive to arrive there. Introduce Xero to your staff during the months when you are experimenting with it. Plan on training them in its basic functions and in all the ways that it can automate your workflow. Encourage, or even require, your staff to earn Xero certification.

When you begin providing Xero services to your clients, start slow and measure your progress. Some firms begin by giving each staff member one Xero account. Schedule regular meetings (we have them each week) to talk about how it can add value to your services, and the best practices for achieving that goal. These meetings are also an excellent opportunity to review Xero accounts and financial statements; be sure to emphasize the valuable insights these reports provide, and what those insights can mean to your clients. With the orientation toward evaluating workflow that you began while getting started with Xero, you can begin building your firm's own Xero knowledge base, which would be a repository of best practices, tips, and time-saving tricks.

5. Select Your Service Offerings and Target Industries

This is where the groundwork you laid in scrutinizing your workflows begins to pay off. That exercise (which you really should incorporate as an ongoing practice) can provide insights to what you do well and where you can become more efficient. Each firm will have an individual set of service offerings that represent your greatest potential for providing greater value to your clients. Figure out what those service offerings are, and focus on them. Your firm will never be the perfect solution for every potential client. Understand what your strengths are, and develop your expertise with them. They may be bookkeeping and payroll, or they may be outsourced controllership or CFO services. Whatever they are, organize your practice around them, and communicate to your clients that you can do these things better, and provide more value for your fee, than anyone else.

Of course, it's not *all* about your service offerings; you offer those services to clients, after all. So identify the clients to whom you can provide the most value. If they are in retail or e-commerce, focus on those industries. If you are better with professional services clients, go for attorneys and physicians. The point here is just that if you serve clients who are in businesses that you genuinely like and/or understand, you will be much better at doing your job, be more efficient, and ultimately make more money.

6. Standardize Project Management

This is another step in understanding and standardizing your practice at a granular level. After you have identified the service offerings you will be specializing in, go back and evaluate all the tasks that go into each of those offerings. The point here is to standardize those tasks so that you can assign them to specific individuals on your staff. They in turn will understand those tasks explicitly so that they can complete them expertly and in a timely way. To keep track of all those tasks being completed, and to improve workflow efficiency, you will need a project management tool. Obviously, you should look for a cloud-based tool that integrates well with Xero. This will allow you not only to monitor and manage all the work your firm is doing, but also to scale up your client list and distribute your staff over an increasingly large area.

7. Adopt Transparency

Another advantage of a project management system is that you can configure it to allow everyone in your firm to see the status of their projects and how the company is doing. This adoption of transparency brings with it a higher standard of accountability. High-performing teams will see their path to become even higher performing. It also provides a reference for your weekly status meetings, and a way for everyone to understand how your firm generates income and profit. Staff members will be able to understand why they are hitting their targets, or not. Identifying clients who ought to be fired will become easier.

Creating a transparent shop can open your staff's eyes to how they contribute to, or take away from, your bottom line. Typically, this encourages just about everyone to embrace the new paradigm all the more. So open up your books in a summary way. Show the staff your revenues and costs by type. This gives them more "ownership" in the firm and a stronger incentive to make it more productive. You can even make that ownership more tangible through a profit-sharing plan. Partners in most firms that incorporate profit sharing are surprised at the productivity gains that can result from this.

8. Go to Fixed or Value Billing

Billing by the hour has certain disadvantages. First, it assumes that what you're selling is your time, when in fact what you're selling is your skill and the value you provide to your clients. Second, clients don't really care how long it takes you to do something, as long as they have the results in a timely fashion and that they see the value from their perspective. What they care about is the value of your services compared to your fees. Third, no one likes the prospect of receiving a "mystery" invoice, a bill for a quantity not known in advance.

Value billing is a practice that has been more common in law firms. In it, you and your client determine the fee in advance of the work. It is a way of showing your interest in what matters to your client, their needs and expectations, and so it also is a step toward becoming their most trusted advisor. It also allows you to move toward a regular billing cycle, with billing in advance of the service for you, and no surprises for your clients. It also makes it easier to bundle your services, since everyone has a better understanding of the transactions up front.

9. Convert Selected Clients to Xero

We mentioned this back in step three; here we will go into detail. Basically, it's all about giving yourself the best chance to succeed with Xero. So start with just one or a few clients. But how to choose? Good candidates have only a few, simple transactions and workflow. That makes the "before and after pictures" much clearer and understandable to everyone. Transactions and workflows that require a lot of add-ons can tend to blur the picture, and foster confusion rather than confidence. If you have to choose between clients with few-but-complex versus many-but-simple transactions, the clients with simple transactions are the better choice. Xero makes scaling up the volume of transactions easy. With Xero, it is all about the unique transactions, and that is due to the way Xero works with bank rules and cash coding for accountants.

Another way to identify good clients for your first conversions are those for whom you do all the transaction processing, and they have essentially no interaction with the accounting software. But if you have no such clients, or if you do but they are not good candidates for other reasons, be sure that the clients you do choose are comfortable with technology, and understand how they can do better by embracing it.

In any event, transparency will go a long way here, too. Show these clients just how Xero will not only facilitate your providing them with more value, but also reduce their uncertainty and the time it takes for your services. If one or more of these clients is involved with their accounting software, you can provide additional service by migrating their data into Xero and setting up their Xero account. You might be surprised at how positively they respond to this.

10. Work Your Niche (don't just scratch it)

This step circles back to selecting your service offerings and target industries, which together define your niche. Working a niche allows you to serve your clients better than if you tried to generalize. It deepens your understanding of your clients' business issues and the processes you need to perform to address them. Another way of saying this is that it enables you to understand their pain, and having that understanding allows you to provide services to them that no generalist could. Naturally, they will be willing to pay more for the added value of those services, because those services improve their productivity and profitability.

Working your niche also allows you to scale up your volume. As you have established yourself as a specialist, you can attract the business of more clients, across a wider geographic area, in that niche. At the same time, standardized workflows and value billing allows you to be paid more for less effort. What is more, understanding a few, specific industries makes you more valuable as a business-development advisor in those industries—a most trusted kind of advisor. The word-of-mouth about the terrific value you provide will spread, and when that happens, you are already sold.

Final thoughts

Following the guide we have presented in this book will enable you to add a Xero to your accounting practice. Of course we did not include every individual step or contingency, but, from having talked about Xero to as many accountants as we have, we believe that we have given you the basic structure you need to be successful. Also, it's all about specialization, and no one can do that for you.

Still, you are likely to have many questions as you browse the Xero website, experiment with the system, and implement it in your practice. Some of you may be unfamiliar with cloud technology, others may be tentative about doing such things as firing nonproductive clients. The good news is that Xero and the Xero community have a rich supply of support resources, and the ease of Internet research allows you to find reliable ideas addressing the sorts of concerns that embracing the new paradigm can raise.

Although I am confident that using Xero can help you build your firm into a more profitable and/or productive business, I won't claim Xero will make you rich overnight. It took me almost two years, and a lot of preaching to non-choir members, to build my million-dollar Xero practice. There was a lot of networking involved, and a lot of time spent demonstrating to myself and my coworkers the advantages that come together in a Xero practice. It wasn't always a smooth road, but I had a clear view to where I was headed, so while some of the bumps hurt a bit for a little while, they never caused me to change course.

Then again, we didn't have such good guide as you now have. Your mileage may vary, but I'll bet that it will vary in a good way.

Hopefully, by following the guidance offered in this book, along with the stories of the bumps and successes we've shared, you can get started on your path to building a 21st century accounting firm that delivers better client value and provides you with more success. Possibly even more importantly, you'll build a firm that will have significantly better market value when it comes time for you to retire.

.

Appendix: Rod Drury's Webio

Each month, the Sleeter group publishes a "Webio"—a video interview with a new guest who will inspire, educate, and remind you that others have travelled the road to success before you. Rod Drury's Webio was full of insight and inspiration. Watch the full video at www.sleeter.com/webio.

Figure 3 Rod Drury's Interview

Index

Adler, Alfred.............. 43

ADP......................... 77

AffinityLive
...................69, 81, 90

Allen, David.............. 65

API 74

AppRiver............. 36, 94

Apps 73

Bill.com 38, 77, 100

Buffett, Warren 59

Chunkification
...................33, 34, 67

Cloud9 Real Time 99

Collaboration 84, 94

Collaborative
Accounting Services
.... 34, 37

Cosby, Bill 53

Customer Relationship
Management
.... 9, 35, 75, 81, 90

Drucker, Peter............. 5

Drury, Rod
.....v, xi, 2, 20, 76, 109

Economist, The 45

Ecosystem.......37, 73, 75

Einstein, Albert.......... 95

Ernst & Young 12

Expensify................... 77

GoToMyPC 9

Halligan, Tony
.... xii, 14, 16, 89

Harshman Phillips &
Company
. vii, xii, xiii, 2, 12, 26,
35, 40, 55, 62, 68,
69, 81, 92, 97

Harshman, Bill .....xii, 12

Hoffer, Eric............... 21

Horne, Lena 79

InsynQ...................... 99

Intacct.............2, 38, 75

Intuit
2, 9, 25, 34, 37, 38, 76

Kashoo 38

Leadership...................51

LogMeIn...................... 9

Microsoft Dynamics 34

Mobile 34, 38

NetSuite.....................75

Oxford Martin School 45

Pacioli, Luca...............47

Paperless 97

Payroll Relief..............38

Phillips, Bruce . v, vii, x, xii, 1, 12, 26, 35, 40, 50, 55, 62, 68, 75, 81, 92, 97

Project Management 102

ReceiptBank.........76, 77

Right Networks 99

SaaS........... 2, 36, 75, 82

Sage ....ii, 25, 34

Scalability 84

Security...............10, 82

Seneca.......................31

Servers 98

Shopify 77

Sleeter, Doug . v, vii, x, 7, 23, 33, 99, 109

SmartVault............... 68

Specialization 61, 62

StitchLabs 77

SurePayroll............... 38

TiVo......................... 46

Transparency...........103

UniData.................... 99

Value billing.............104

Wave 38, 45

White, E.B. 71

Windows Remote Desktop 9

Xcentric 99

Xero v, vii, ix, 2, 12, 55, 62, 73, 81, 97, 99, 104

Xero Touch............... 40

ZenPayroll ...38, 77, 100

Zero Entry 33, 37